RELAXING FLOWERS
COLORING BOOK FOR ADULTS

Copyright © 2022 by Happy Sophie Press
All rights reserved. This book or any portion thereof
may not be reproduced or used in any manner whatsoever
without the express written permission of the publisher
except for the use of brief quotations in a book review.

First Printing, 2022
Happy Sophie Press

Created by
Evgeniya Khrenova
evgeniya_hrenova@bk.ru

Inspirational Flower Quotes

"Love is the flower you've got to let grow."

Inspirational Flower Quotes

"If you look the right way, you can see that the whole world is a garden."

Inspirational Flower Quotes

"Love is like wildflowers; it's often found in the most unlikely places."

Inspirational Flower Quotes

"Take time to smell the roses."

Inspirational Flower Quotes

"A flower cannot blossom without sunshine, and a man cannot live without love."

Inspirational Flower Quotes

"There are always flowers for those who want to see them."

Inspirational Flower Quotes

"Life is the flower for which love is the honey."

Inspirational Flower Quotes

"What a lonely place it would be to have a world without a wildflower!"

Inspirational Flower Quotes

"I'd rather wear flowers in my hair, than diamonds around my neck."

Inspirational Flower Quotes

"Flowers are a proud assertion that a ray of beauty out values all the utilities in the world."

Inspirational Flower Quotes

"The very best relationship has a gardener and a flower. The gardener nurtures and the flower blooms."

Inspirational Flower Quotes

"The smallest flower is a thought, a life answering to some feature of the Great Whole, of whom they have a persistent intuition."

Inspirational Flower Quotes

"If you tend to a flower, it will bloom, no matter how many weeds surround it."

Inspirational Flower Quotes

"A flower's appeal is in its contradictions — so delicate in form yet strong in fragrance, so small in size yet big in beauty, so short in life yet long on effect."

Inspirational Flower Quotes

"Flowers don't tell, they show."

Inspirational Flower Quotes

"Flowers whisper 'Beauty!' to the world, even as they fade, wilt, fall."

Inspirational Flower Quotes

"Flowers always make people better, happier and more helpful; they are sunshine, food and medicine for the soul."

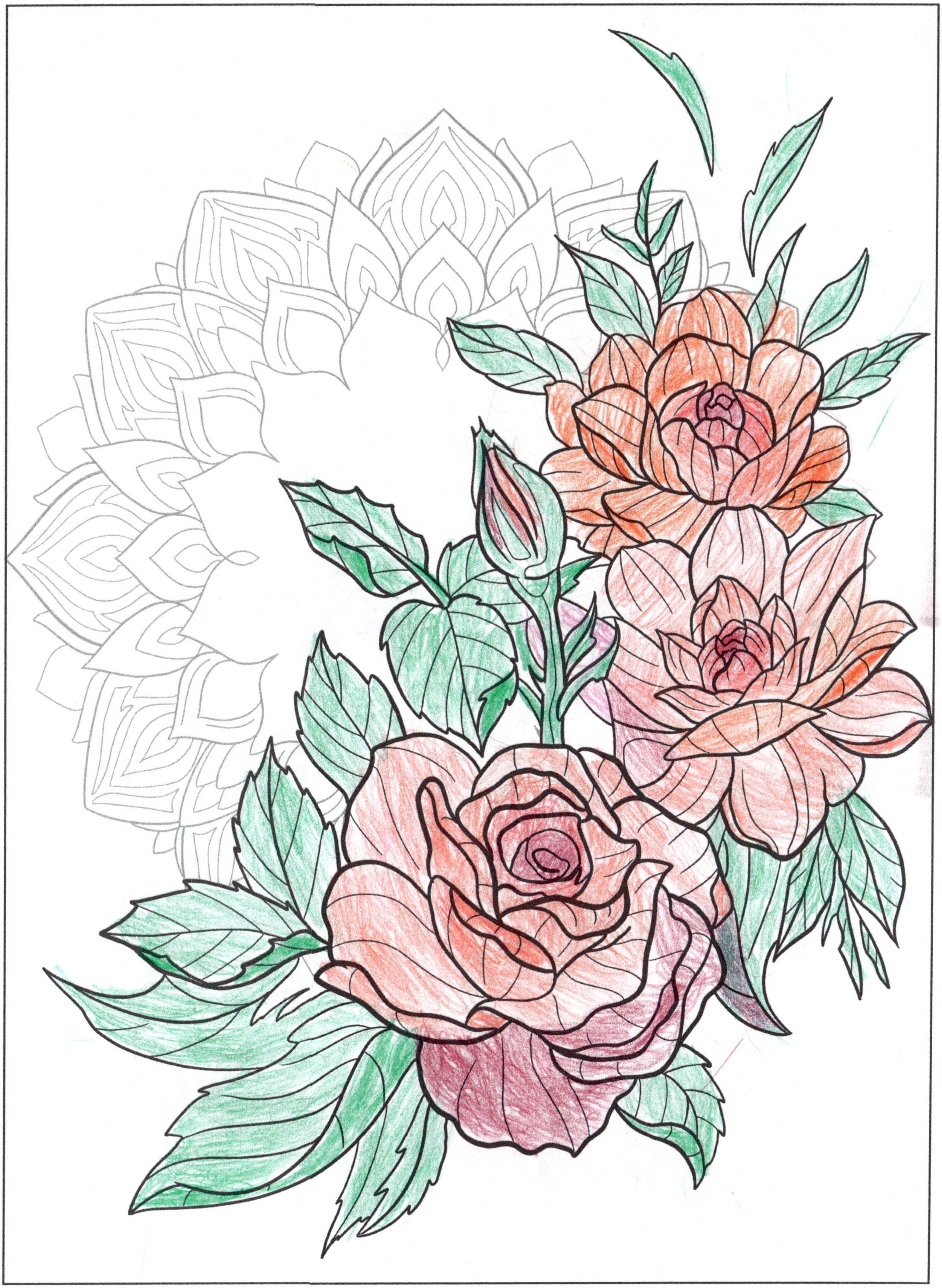

Inspirational Flower Quotes

"You're only here for a short visit. Don't hurry, don't worry. And be sure to smell the flowers along the way."

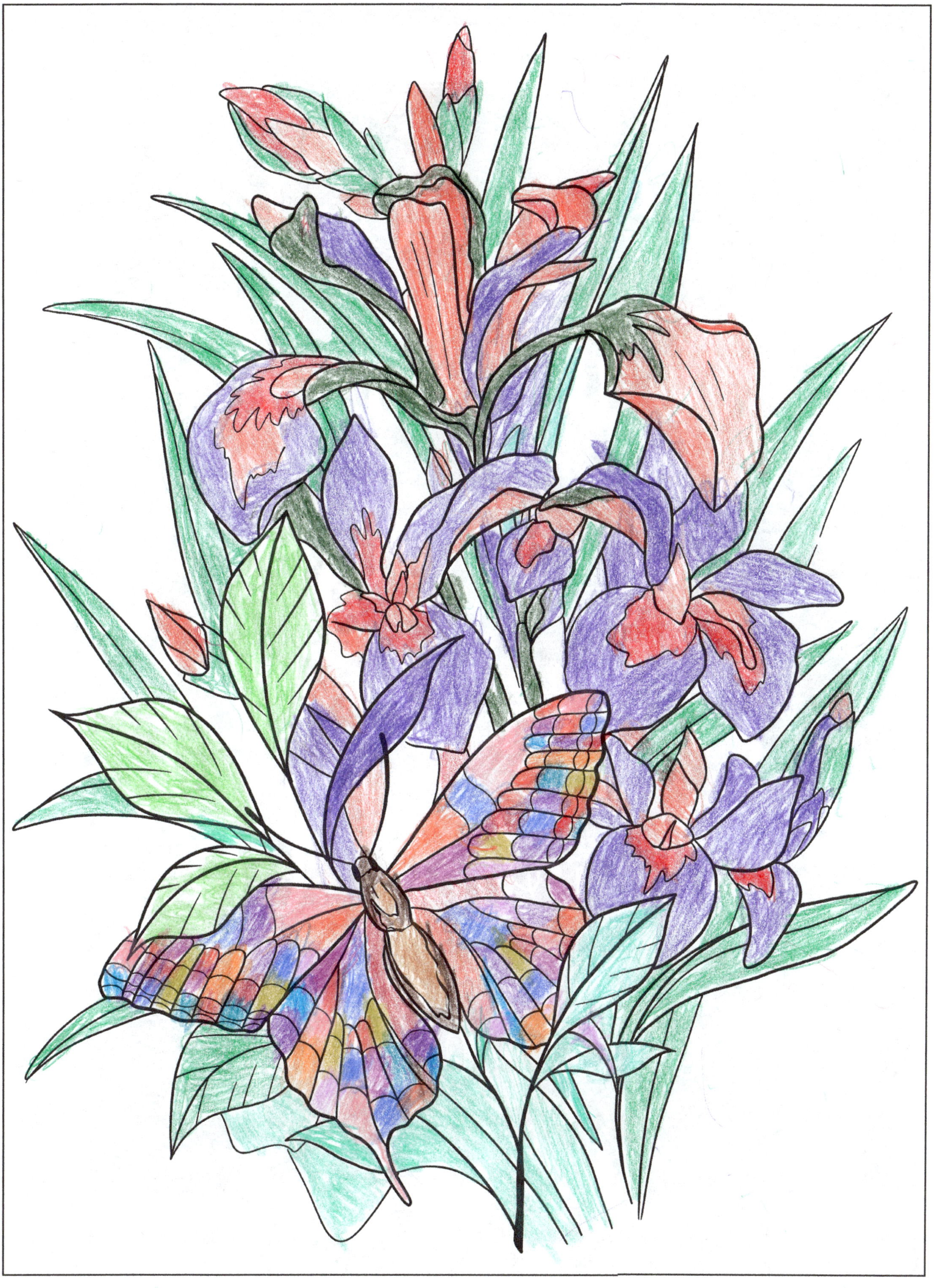

Inspirational Flower Quotes

"If we could see the miracle of a single flower clearly our whole life would change."

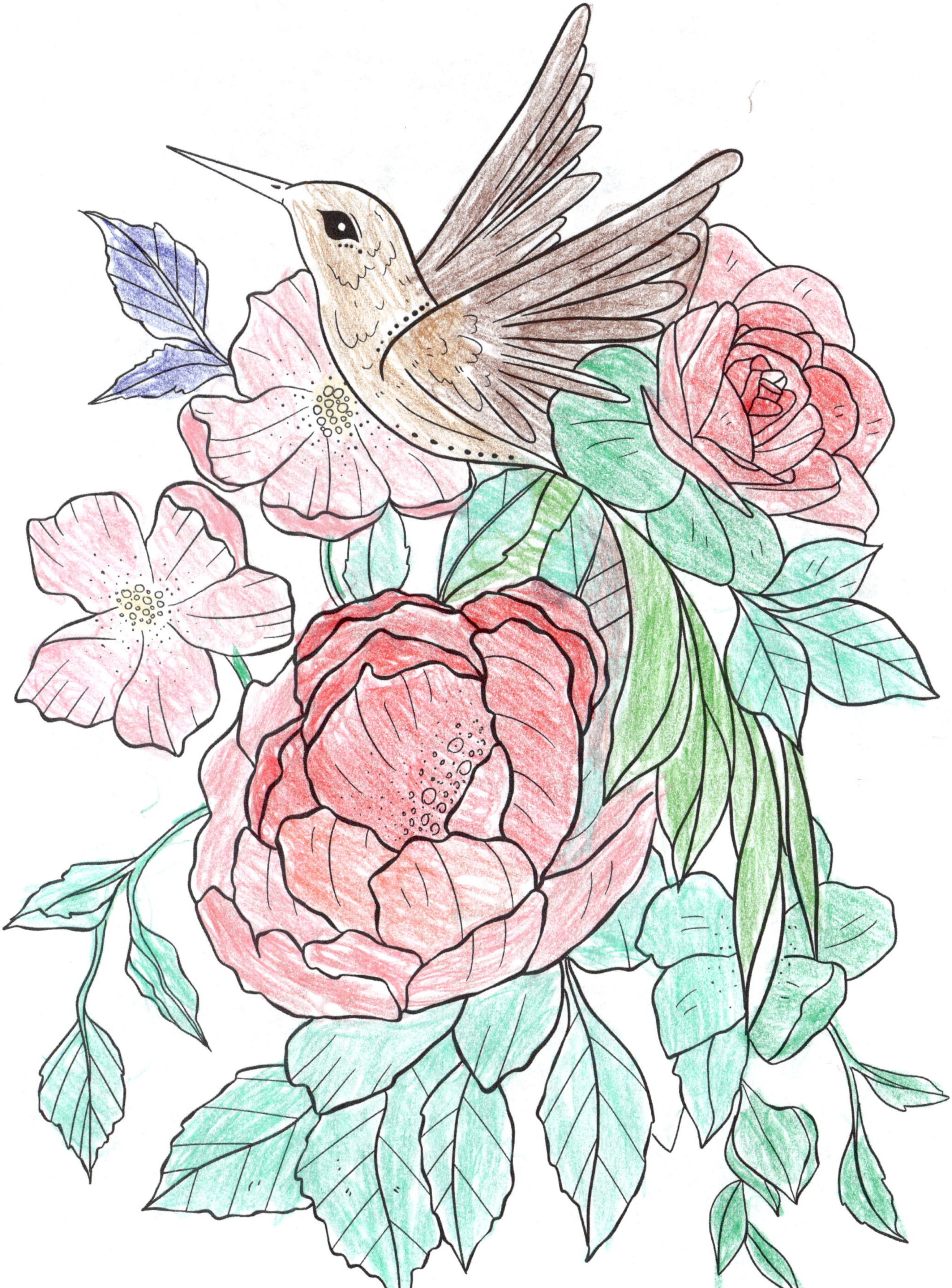

Inspirational Flower Quotes

"My love for you blossoms every day."

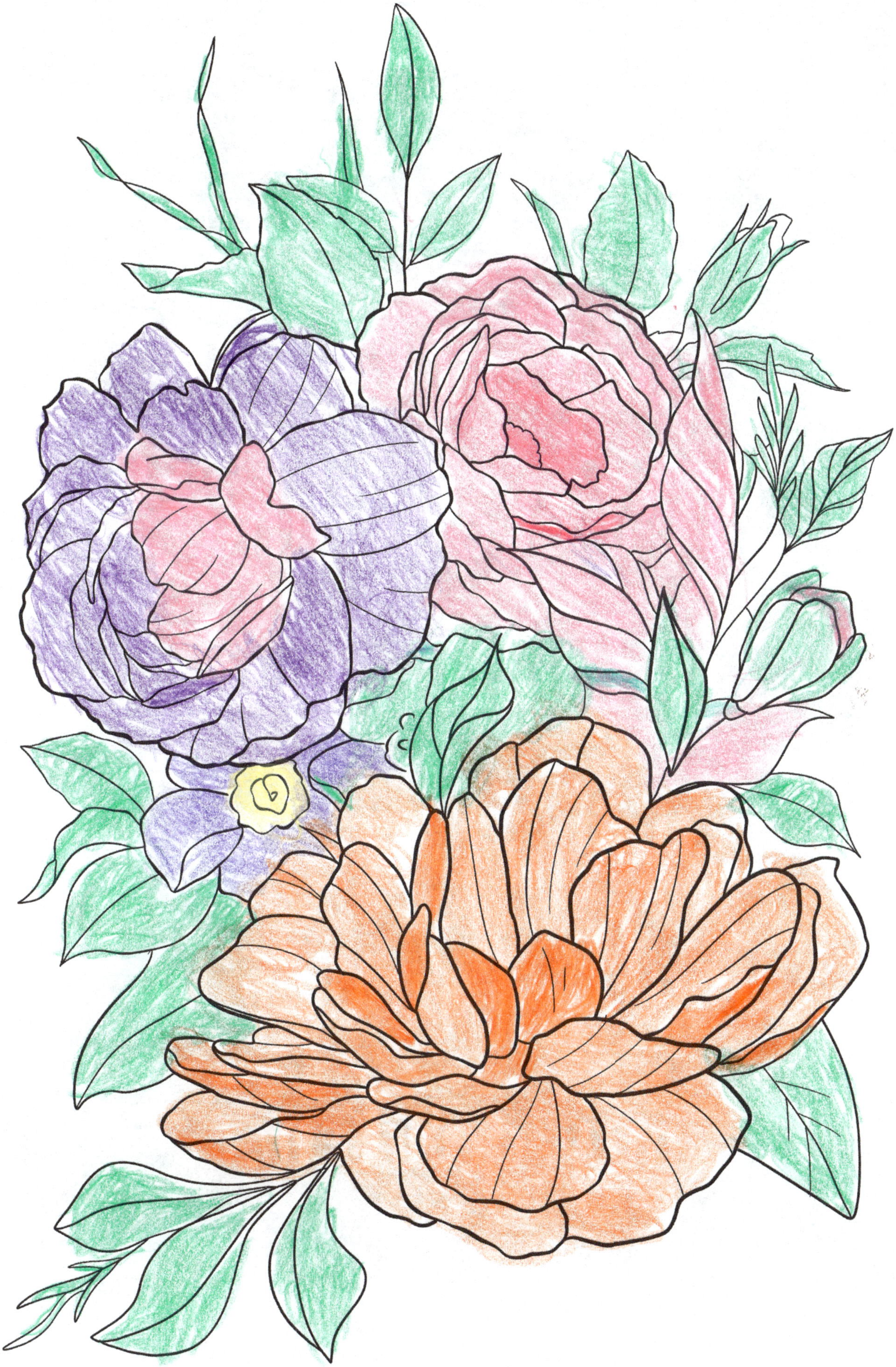

Inspirational Flower Quotes

"If I had a single flower for every time I think about you, I could walk forever in my garden."

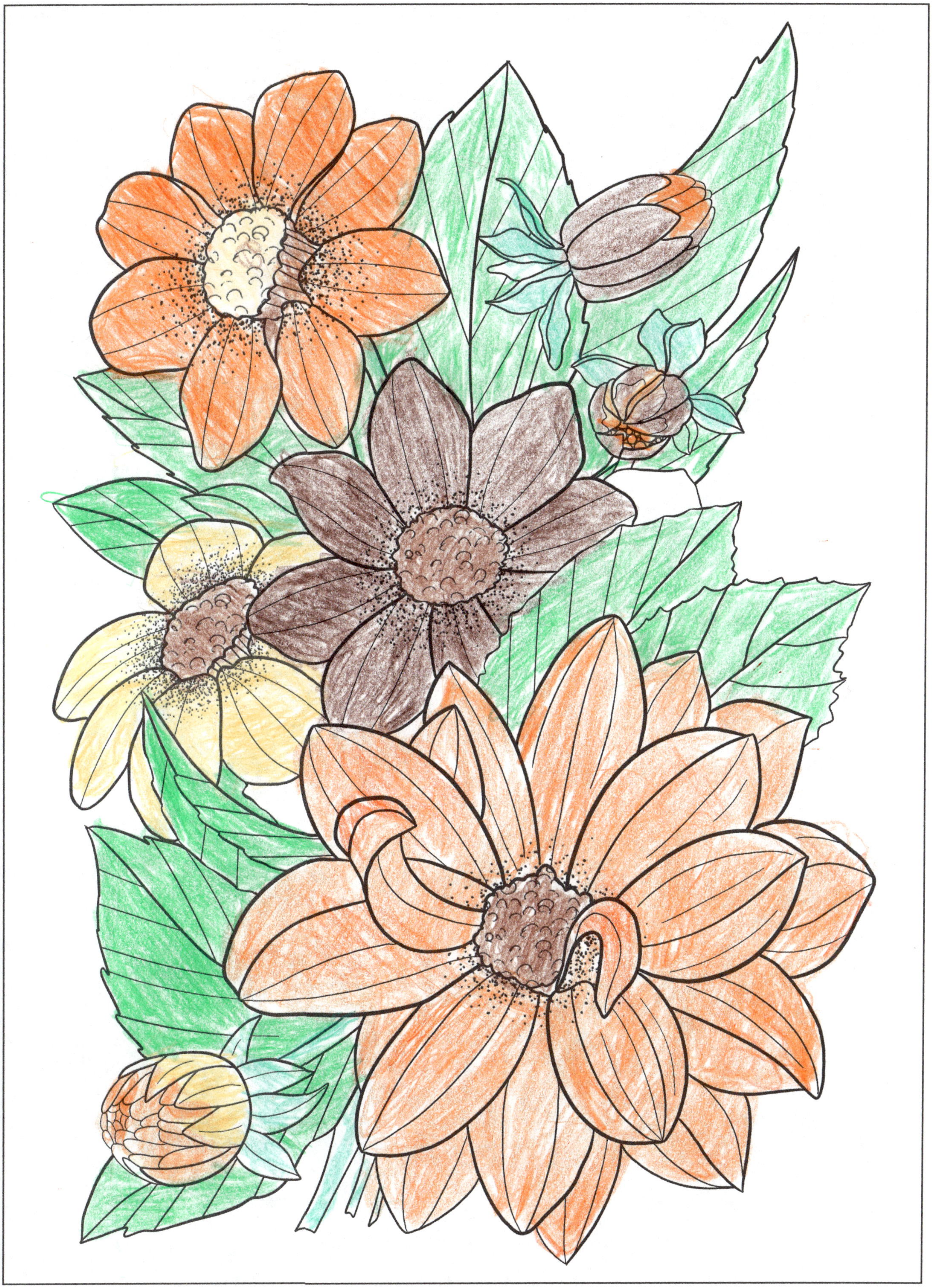

Inspirational Flower Quotes

"All the flowers of the tomorrows are in the seeds of today."

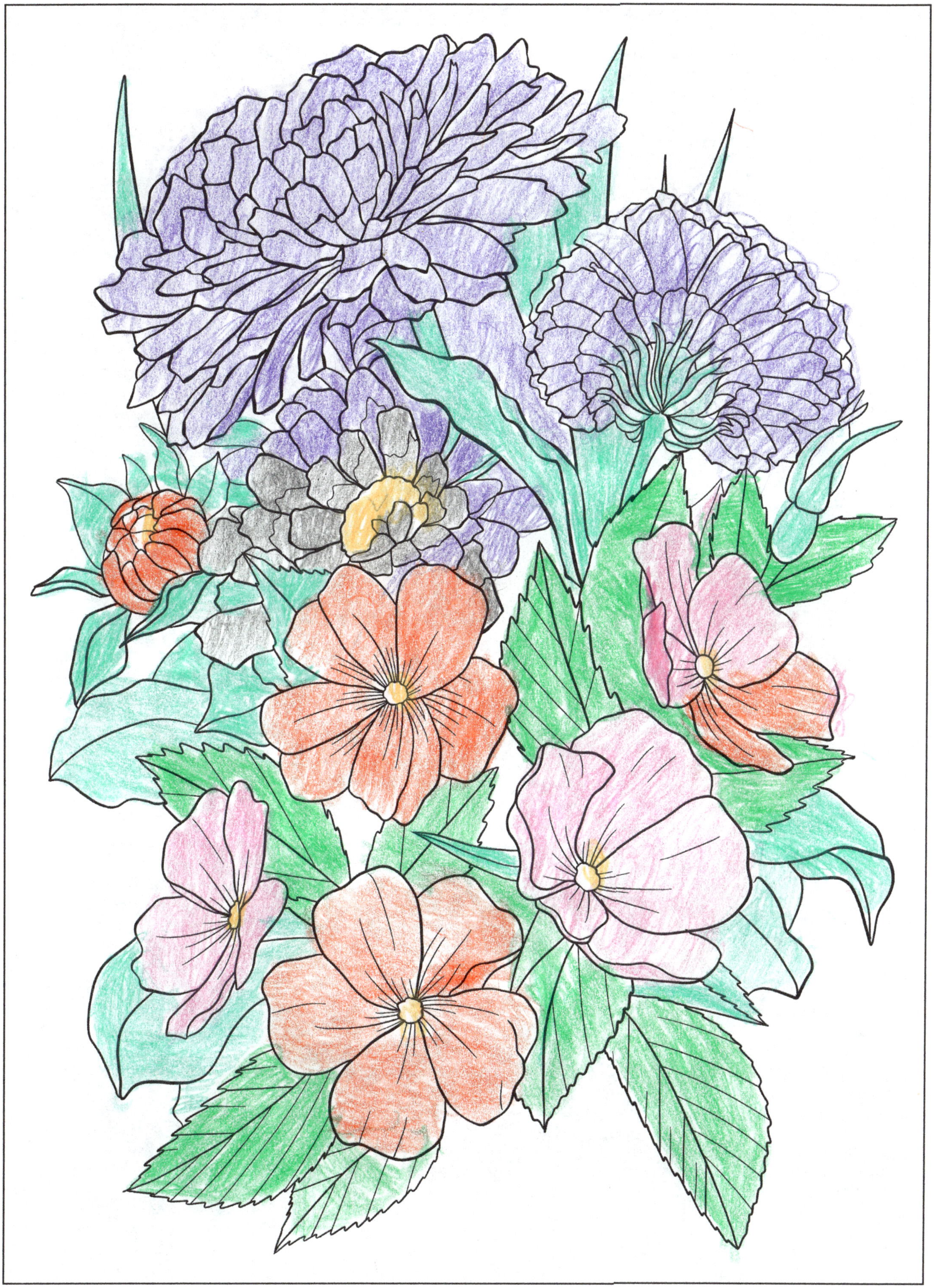

Inspirational Flower Quotes

"Happiness held is the seed; Happiness shared is the flower."

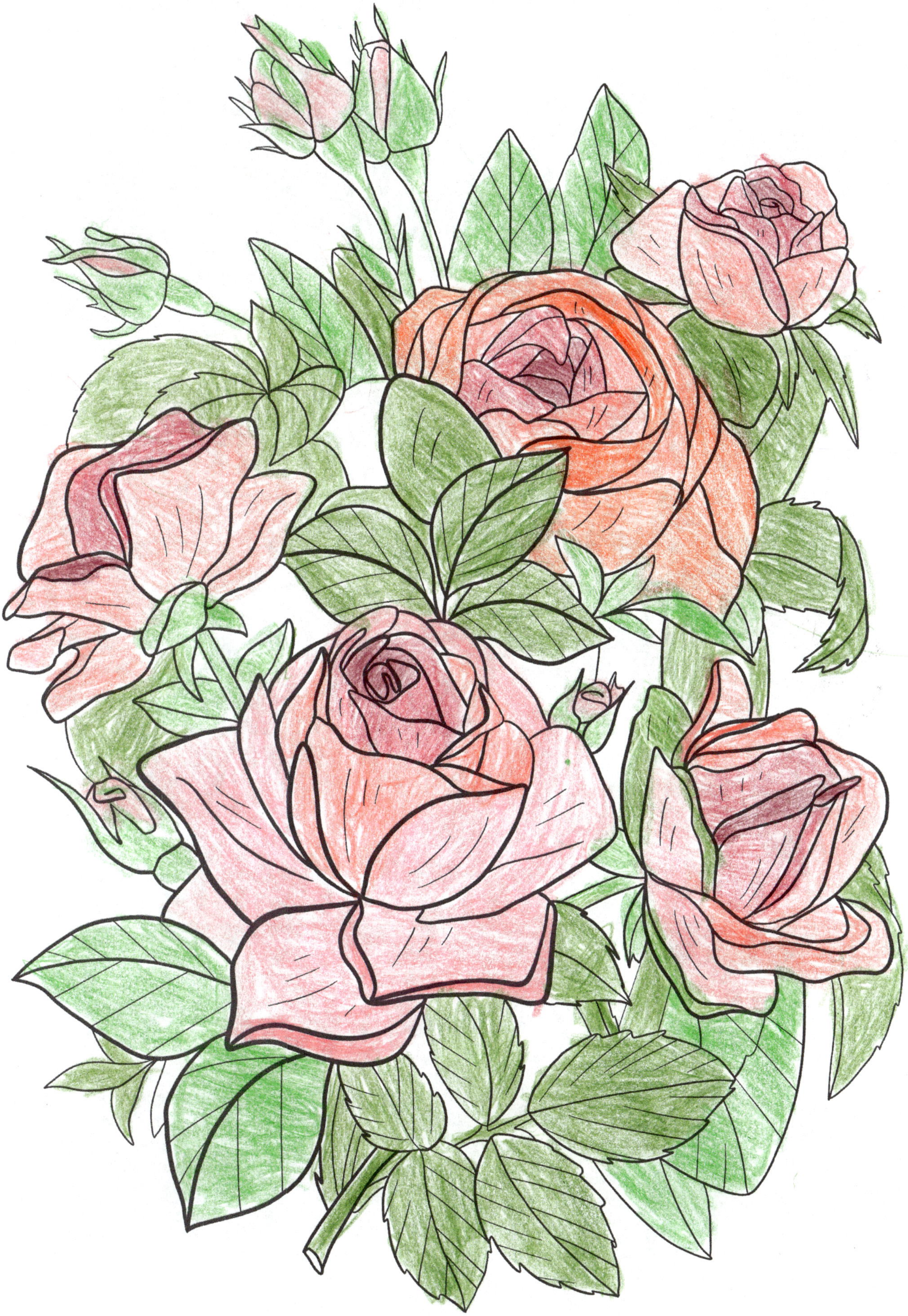

Inspirational Flower Quotes

"Mama was my greatest teacher, a teacher of compassion, love and fearlessness. If love is sweet as a flower, then my mother is that sweet flower of love."

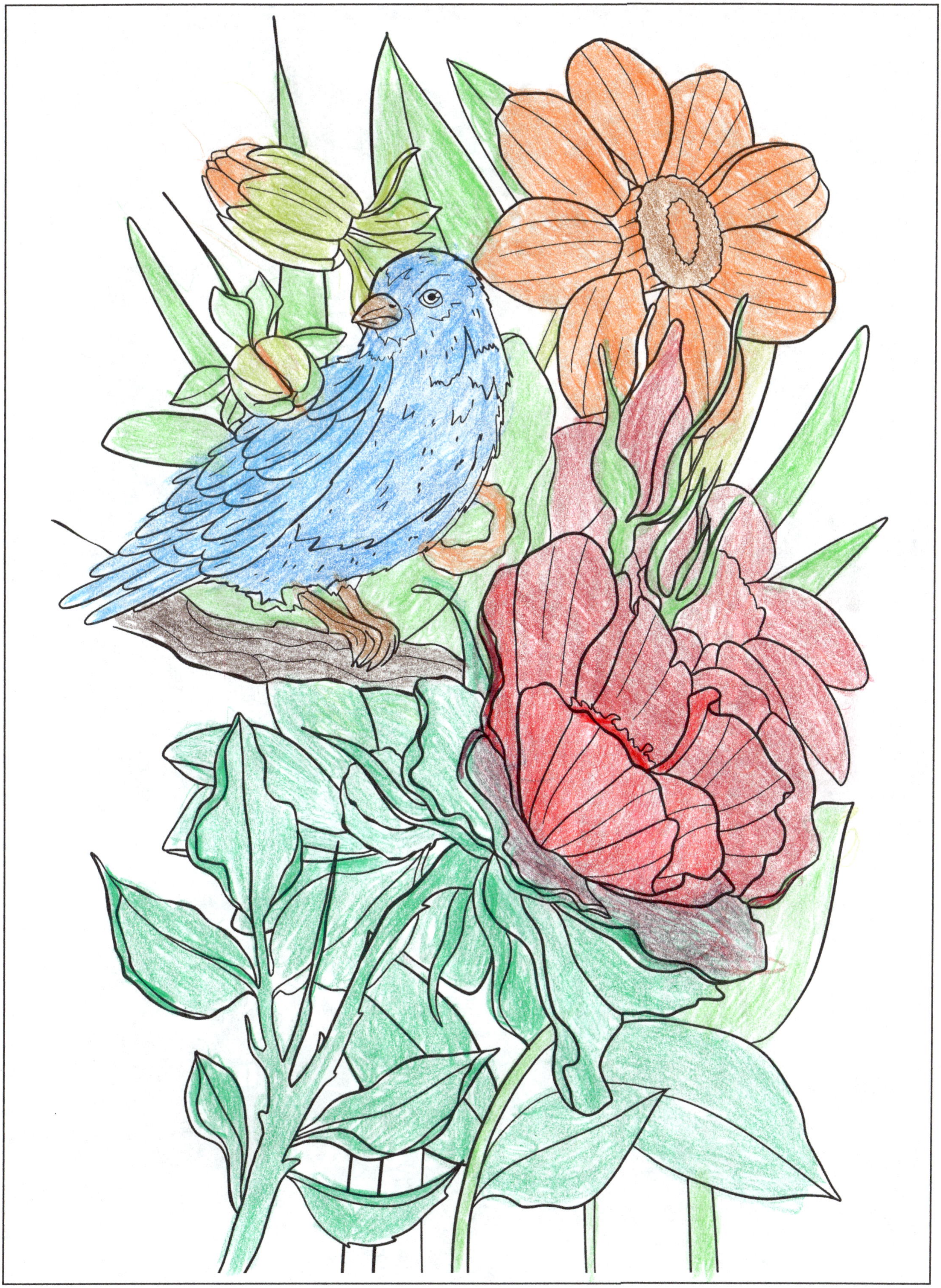

Inspirational Flower Quotes

"The rose is the flower and handmaiden of love — the lily, her fair associate, is the emblem of beauty and purity."

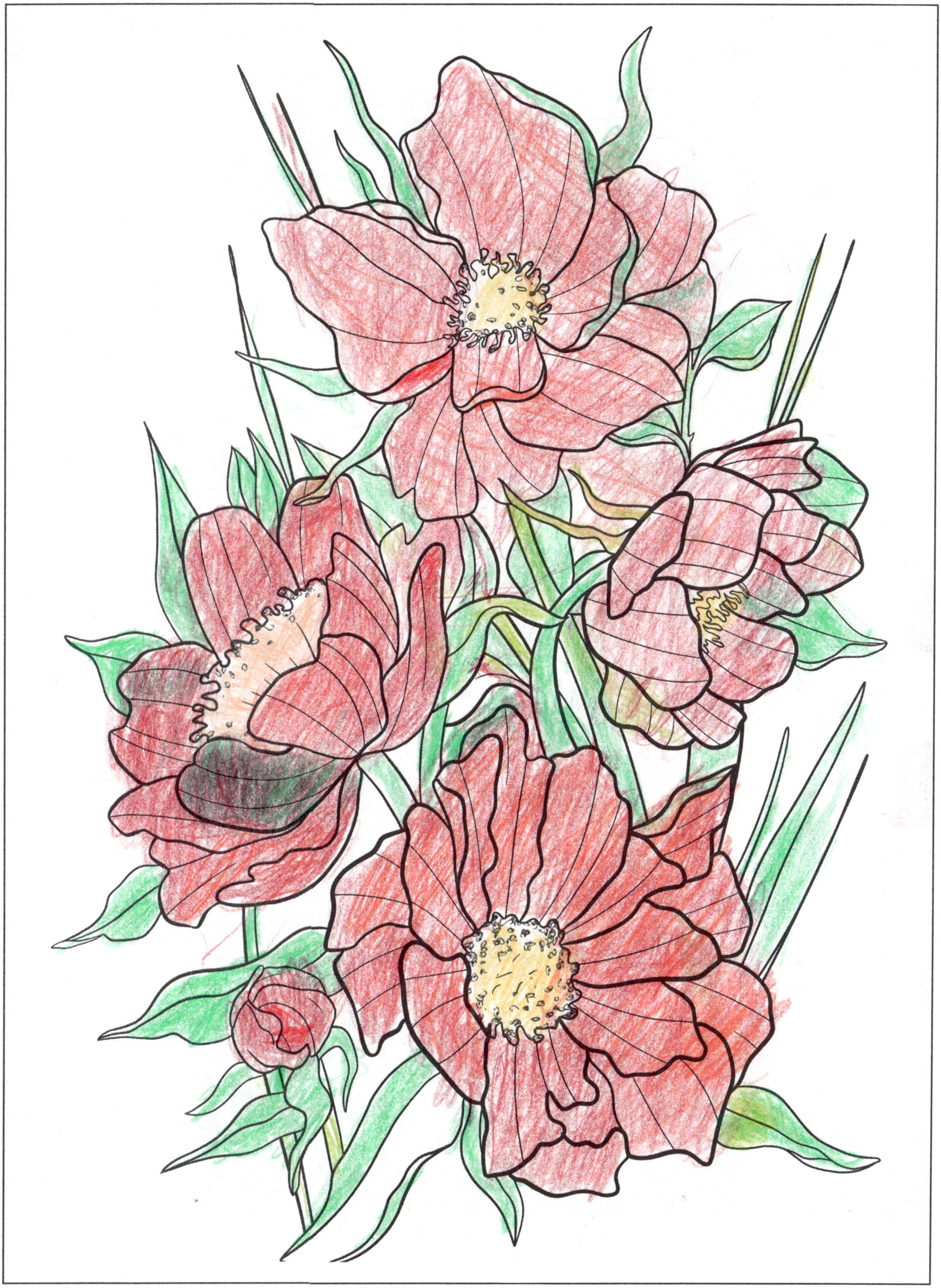

Inspirational Flower Quotes

"She sprouted love like flowers, grew a garden in her mind, and even on the darkest days, from her smile the sun still shined."

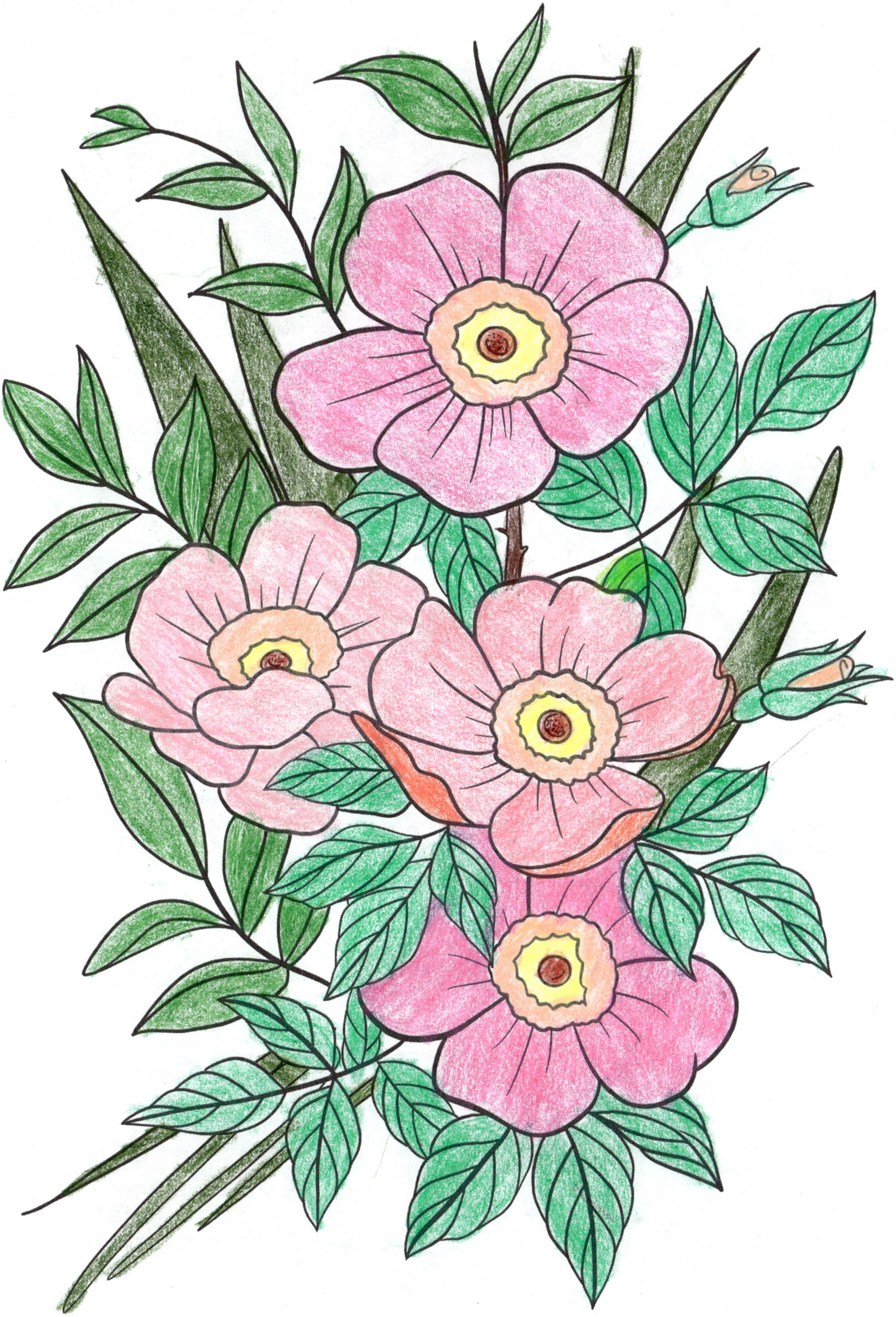

Inspirational Flower Quotes

"Flowers are like friends; they bring color to your world."

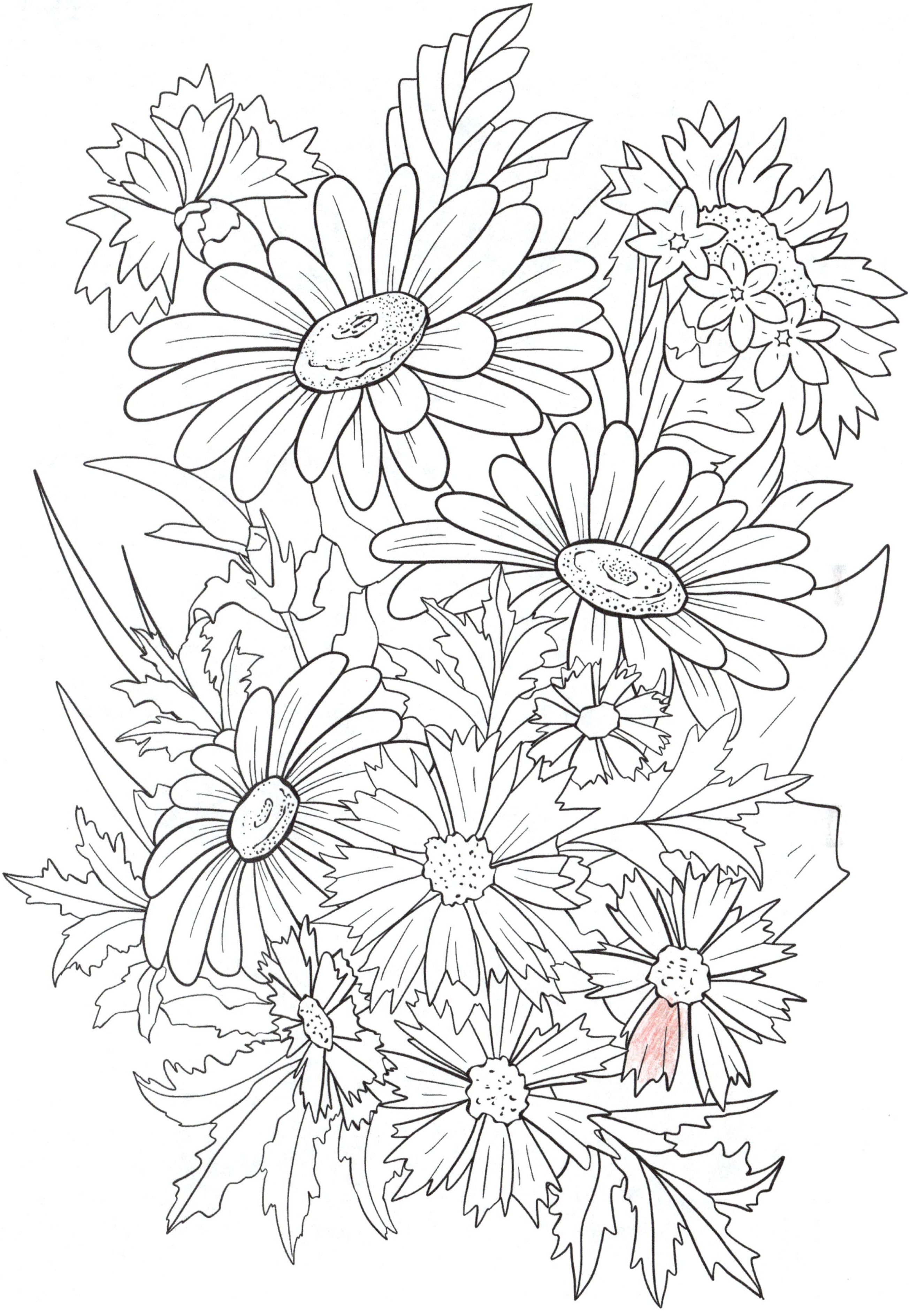

Inspirational Flower Quotes

"She is like a wildflower; beautiful, fierce, and free."

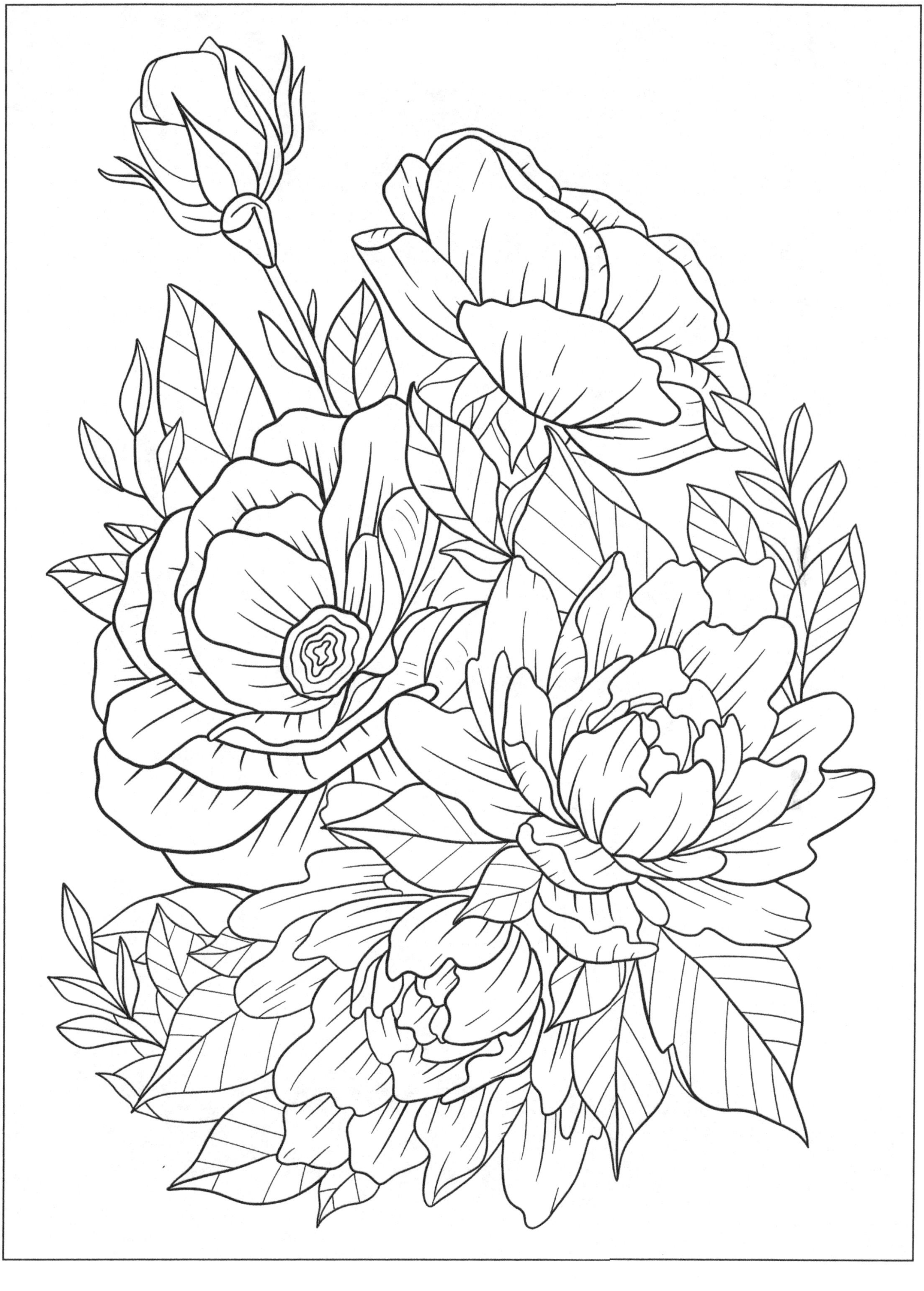

Inspirational Flower Quotes

"Flowers don't worry about how they're going to bloom. They just open up and turn toward the light and that makes them beautiful."

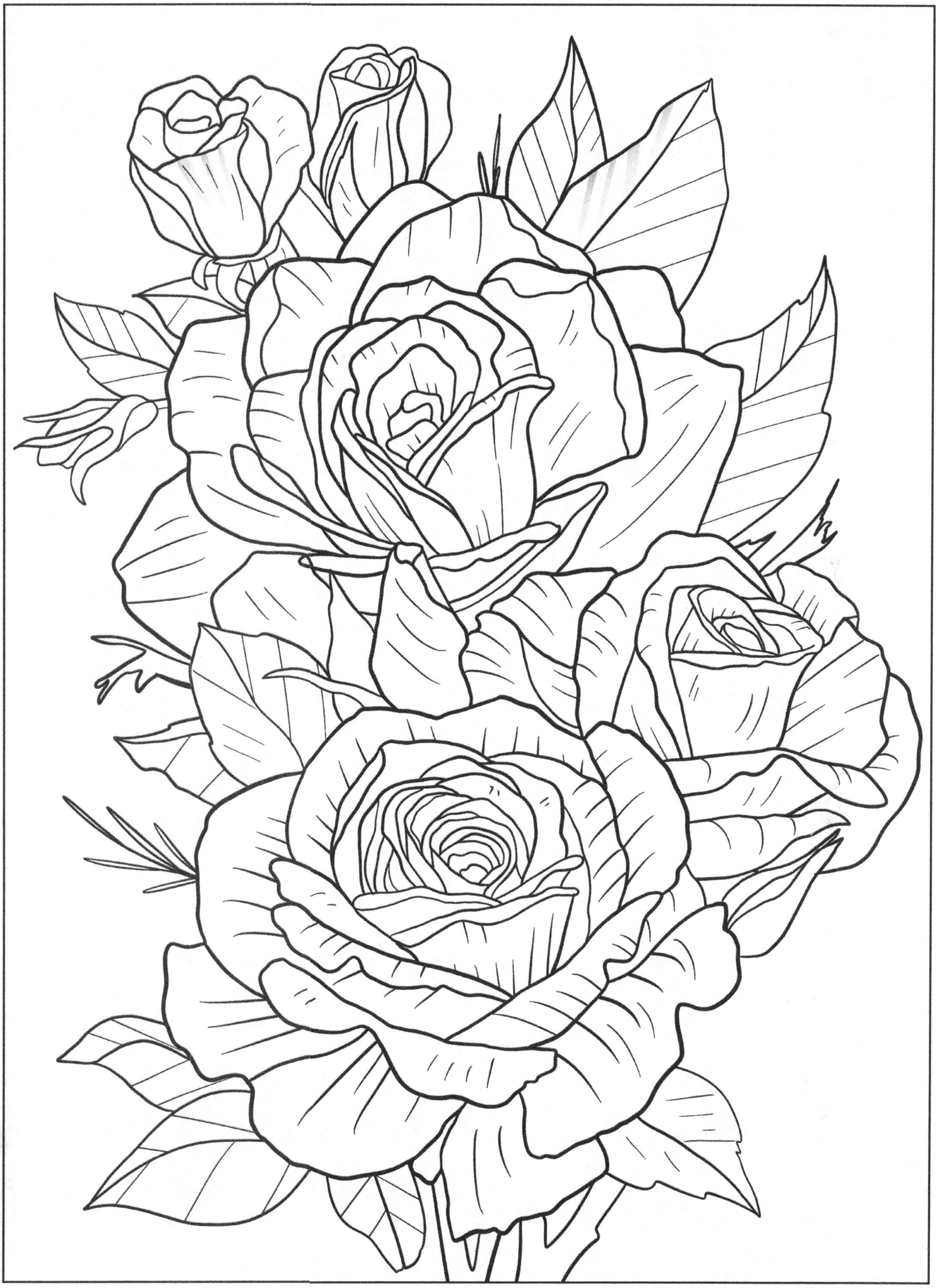

Inspirational Flower Quotes

"Open the bloom of your heart and become a gift of beauty to the world."

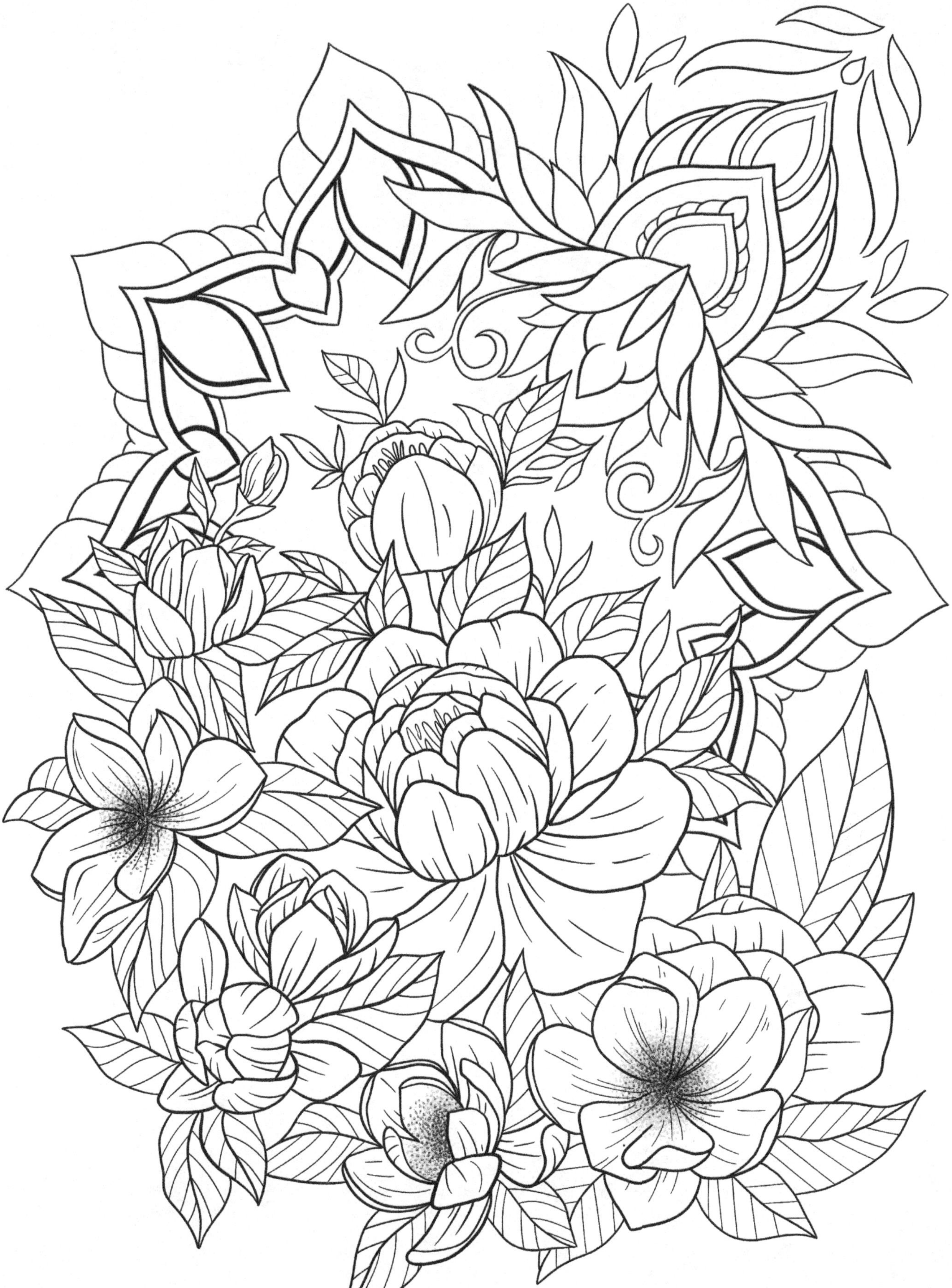

Inspirational Flower Quotes

"Where flowers bloom so does hope."

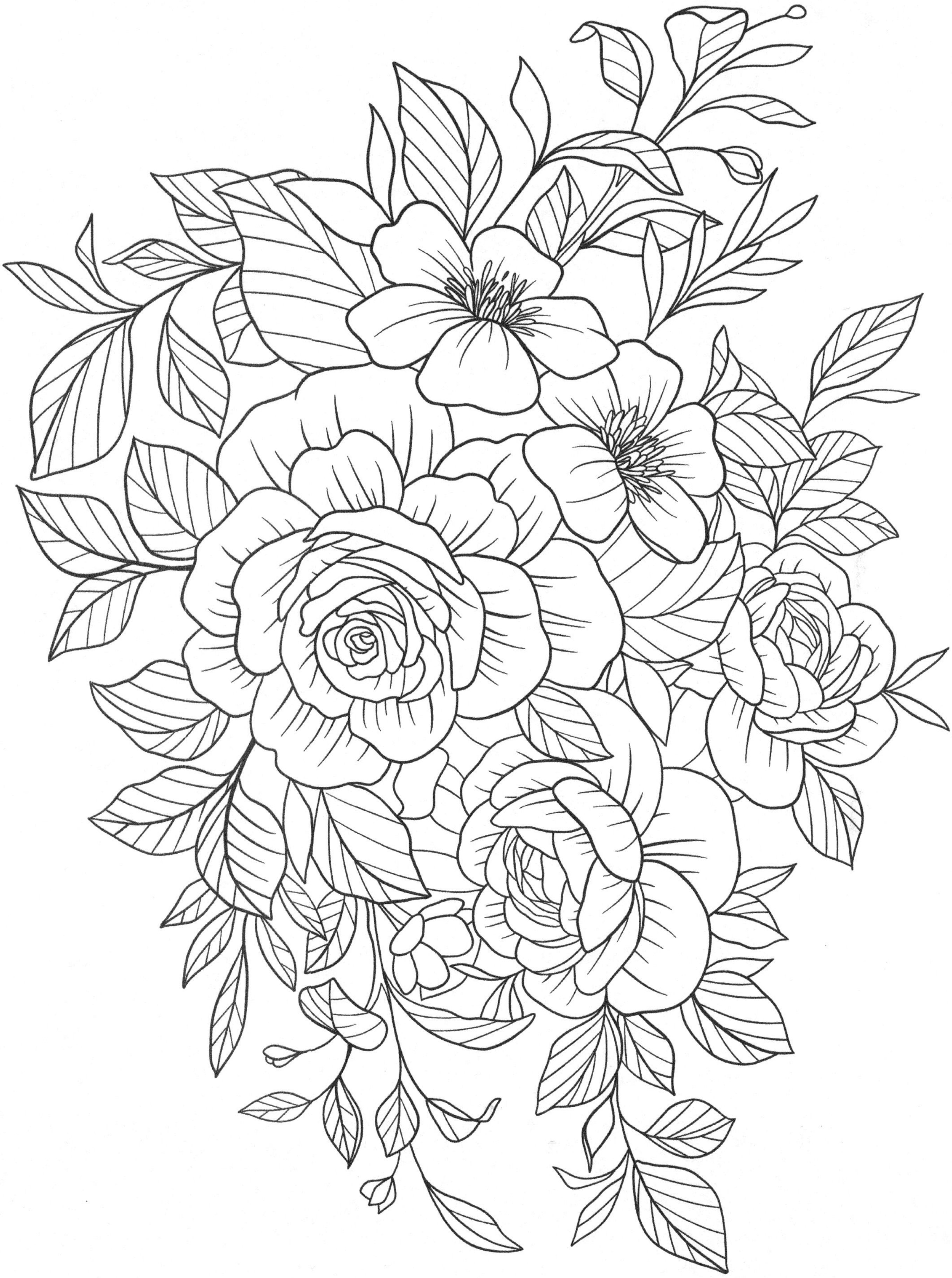

Inspirational Flower Quotes

"Love is flower like; Friendship is like a sheltering tree."

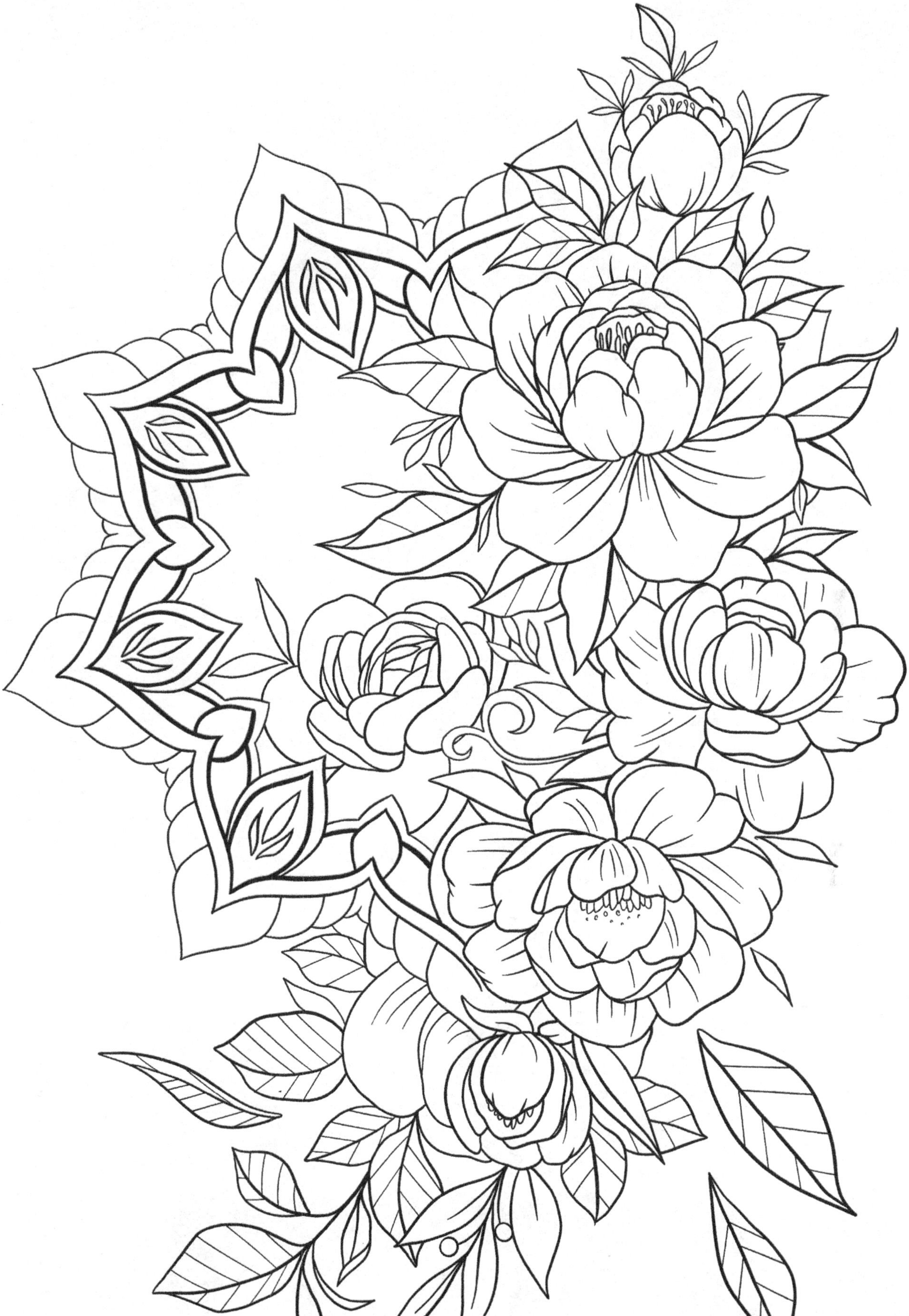

Inspirational Flower Quotes

"A flower does not think of competing with the flower next to it. It just blooms."

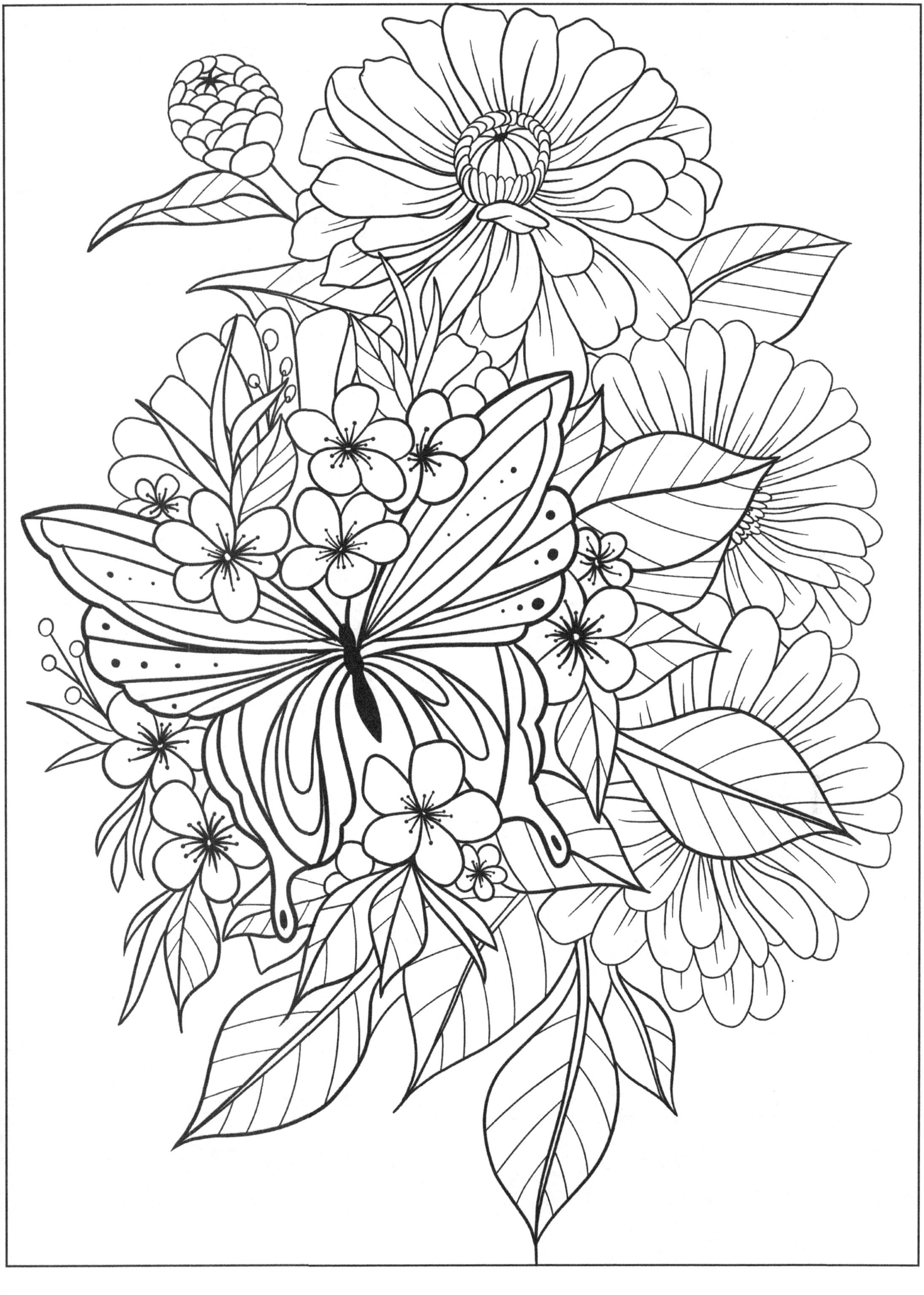

Inspirational Flower Quotes

"Minds are like flowers; they open only when the time is right."

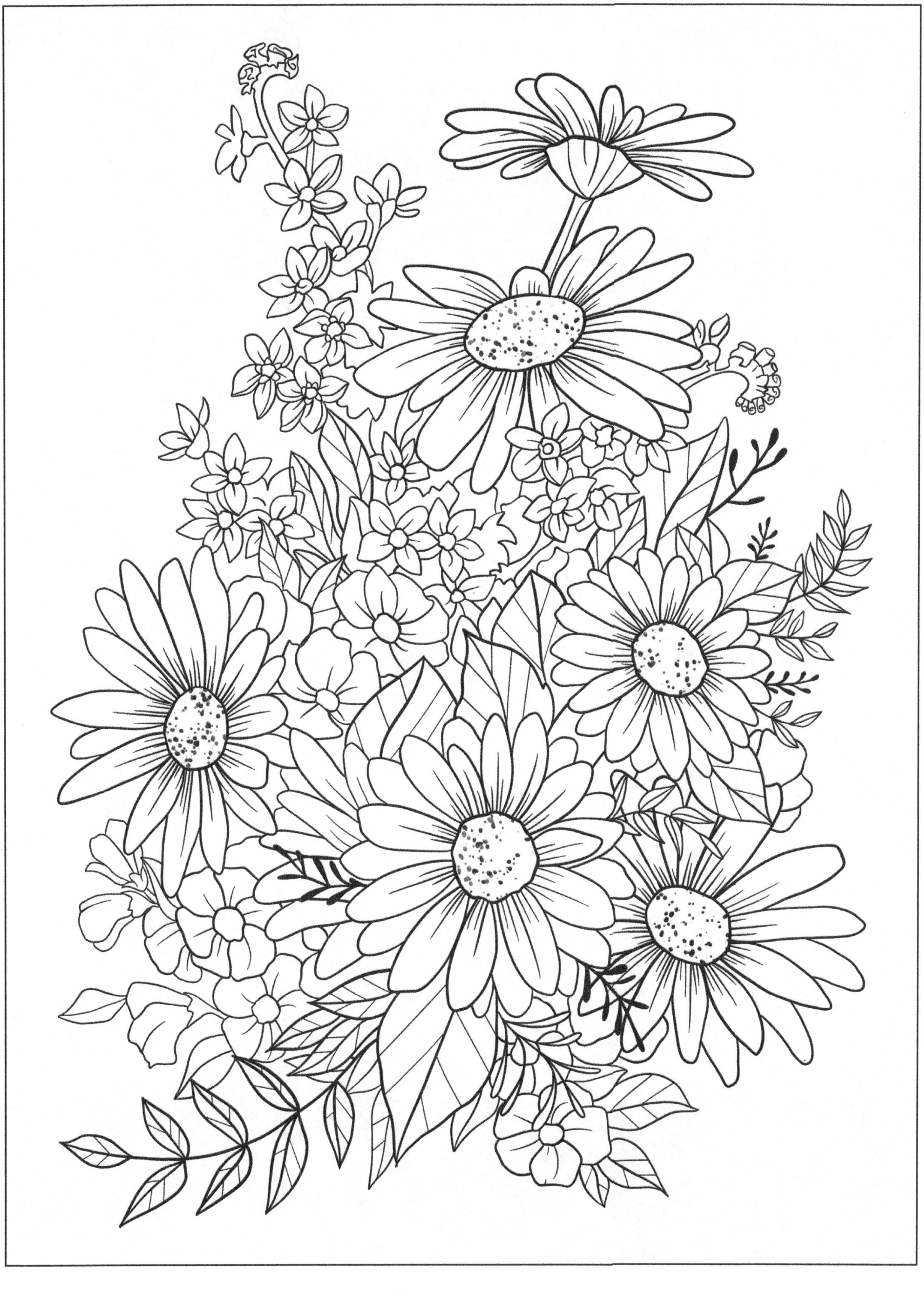

Inspirational Flower Quotes

"Earth laughs in flowers."

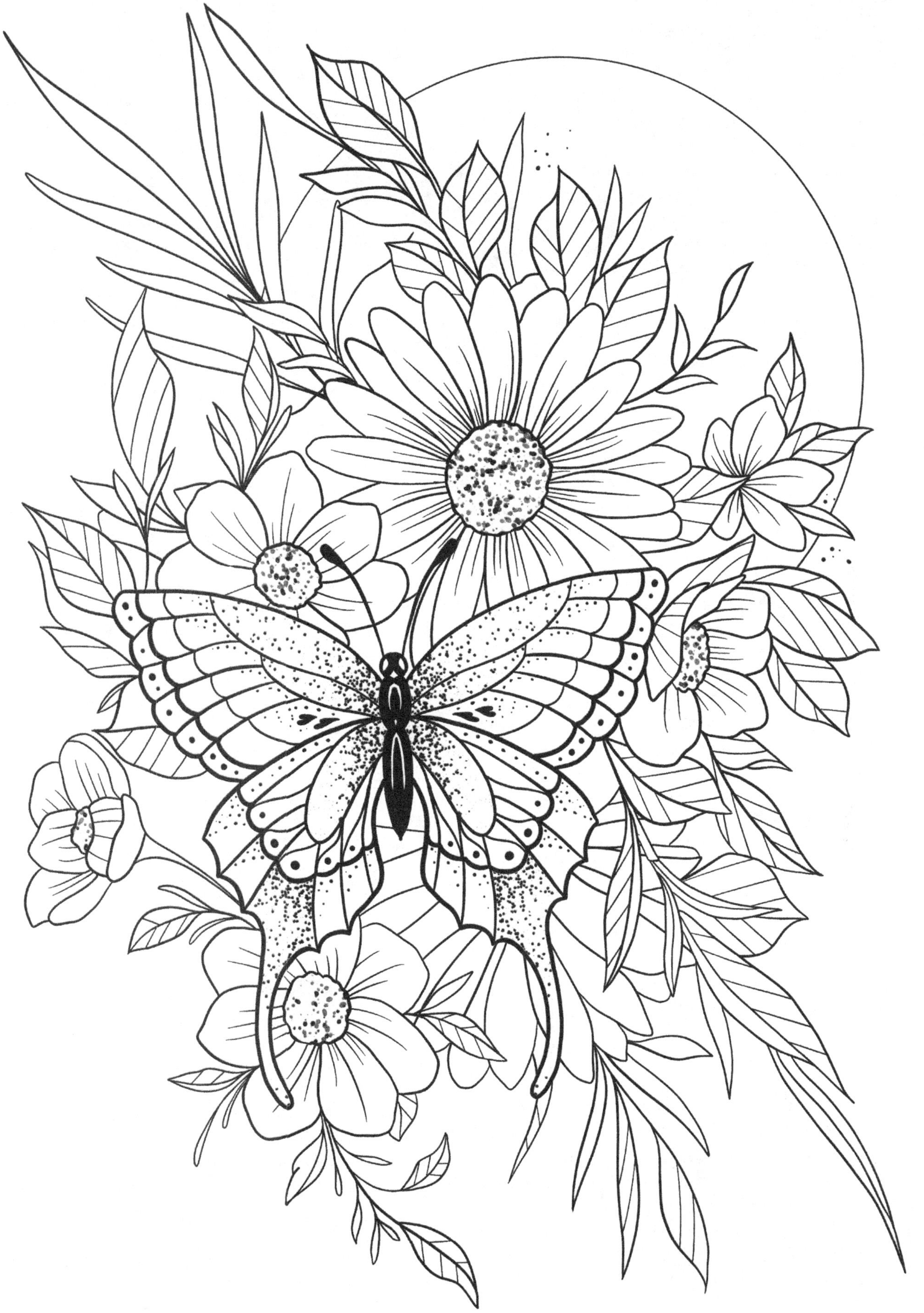

Inspirational Flower Quotes

"The flower that follows the sun does so even in cloudy days."

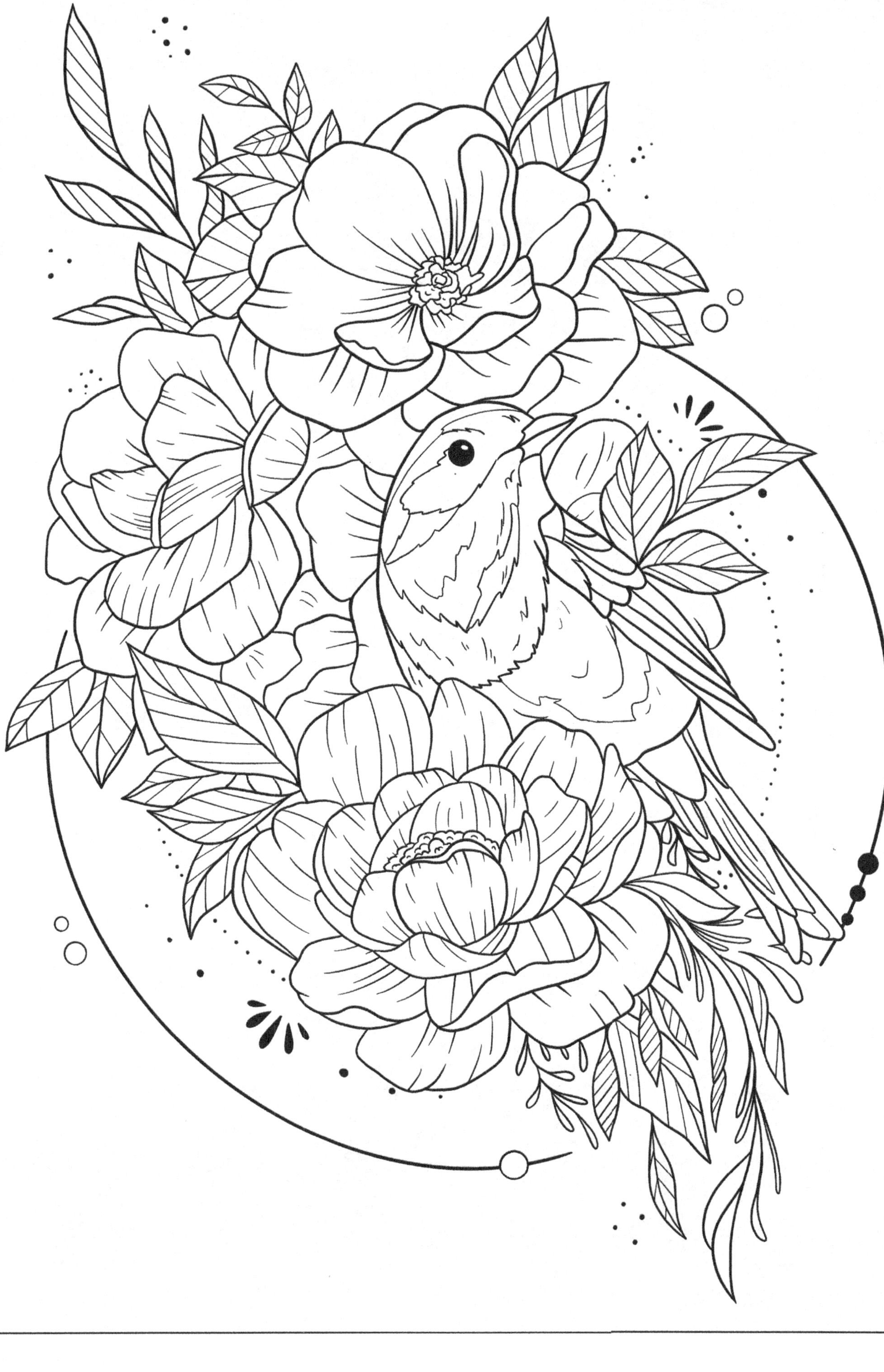

Inspirational Flower Quotes

"Every flower must grow through dirt."

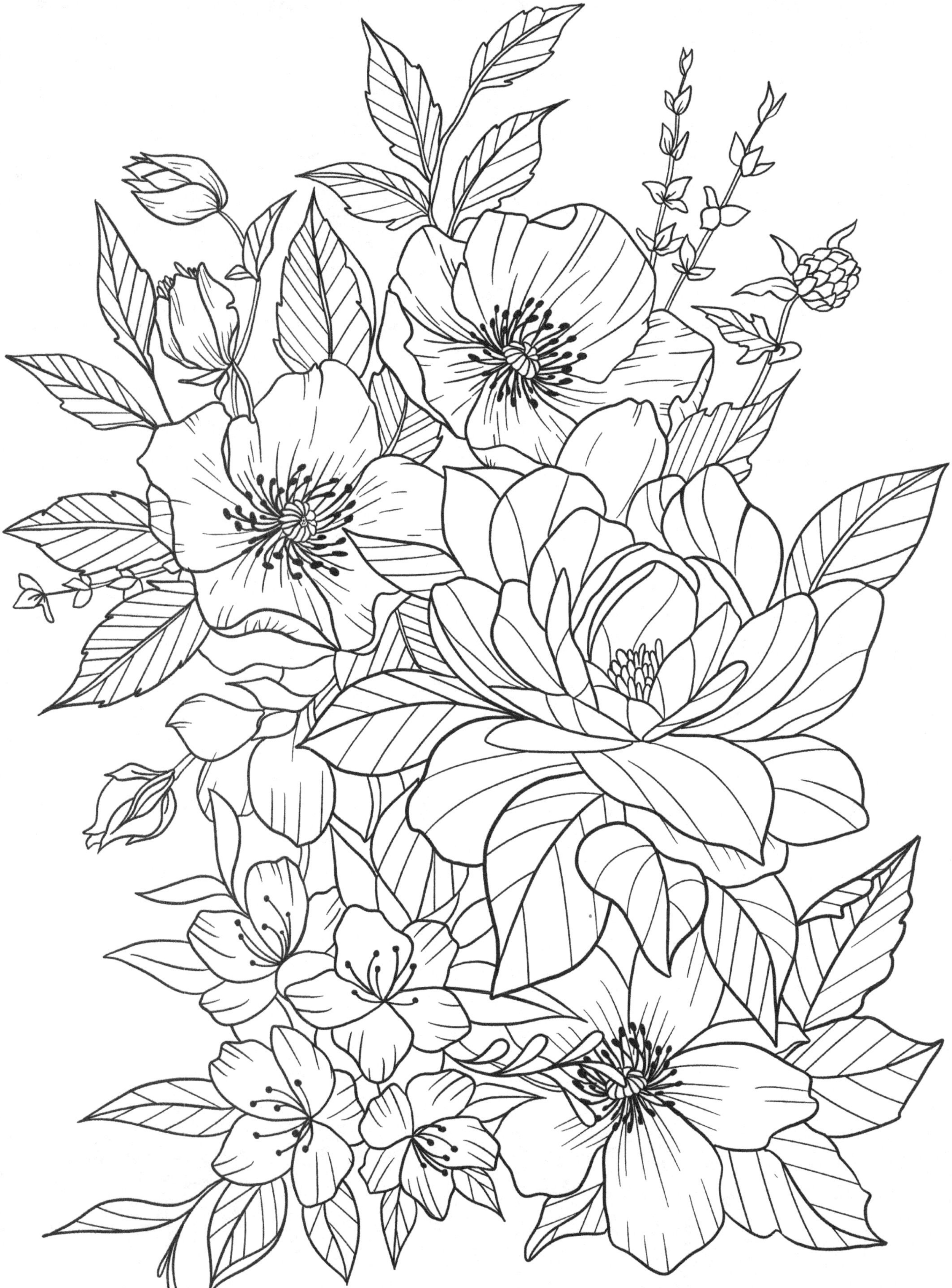

Inspirational Flower Quotes

"Even the tiniest of flowers can have the toughest roots."

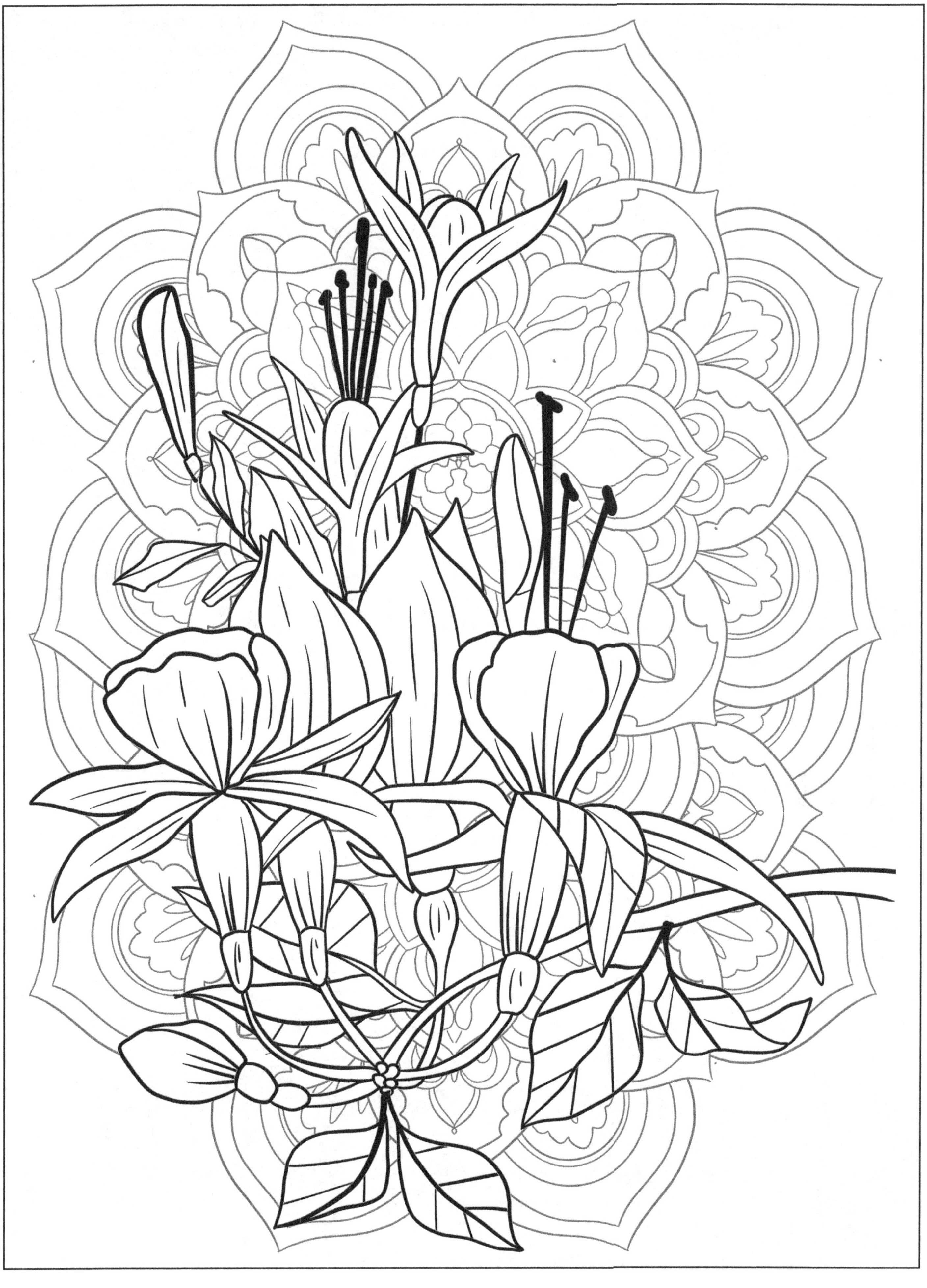

Inspirational Flower Quotes

"Every flower blooms in its own time."

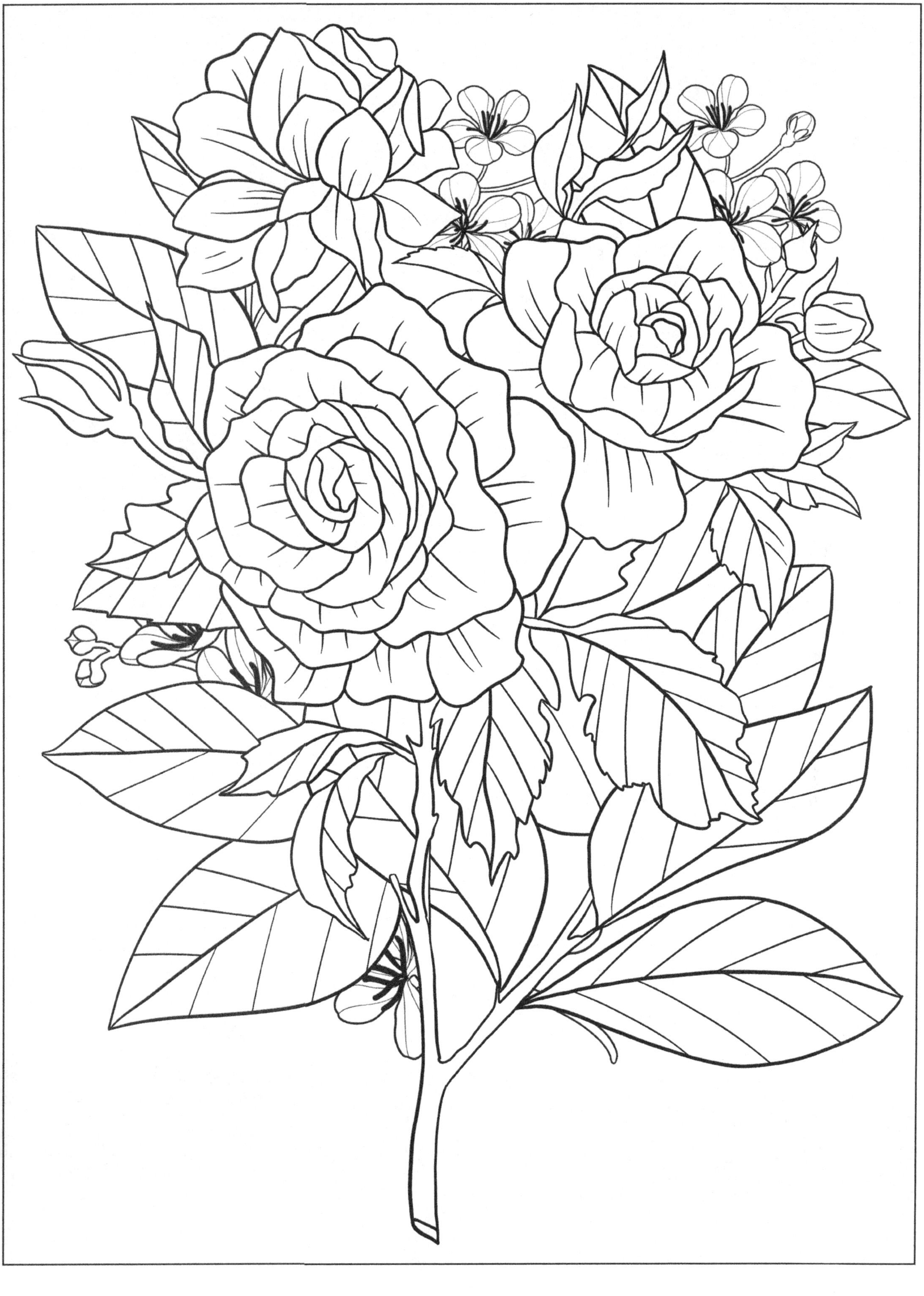

Inspirational Flower Quotes

"The butterfly is a flying flower, the flower a tethered butterfly."

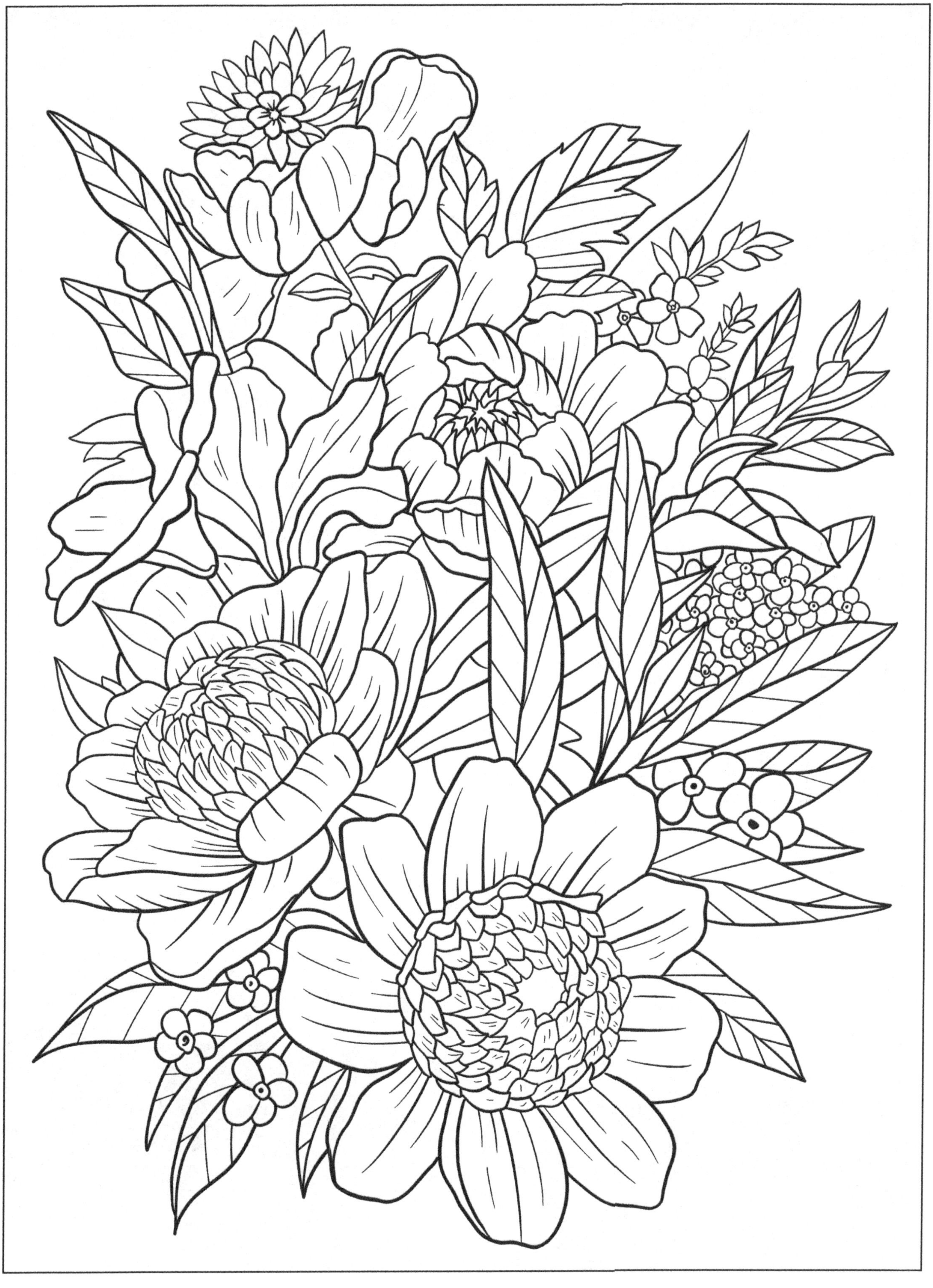

Inspirational Flower Quotes

"Open the bloom of your heart and become a gift of beauty to the world."

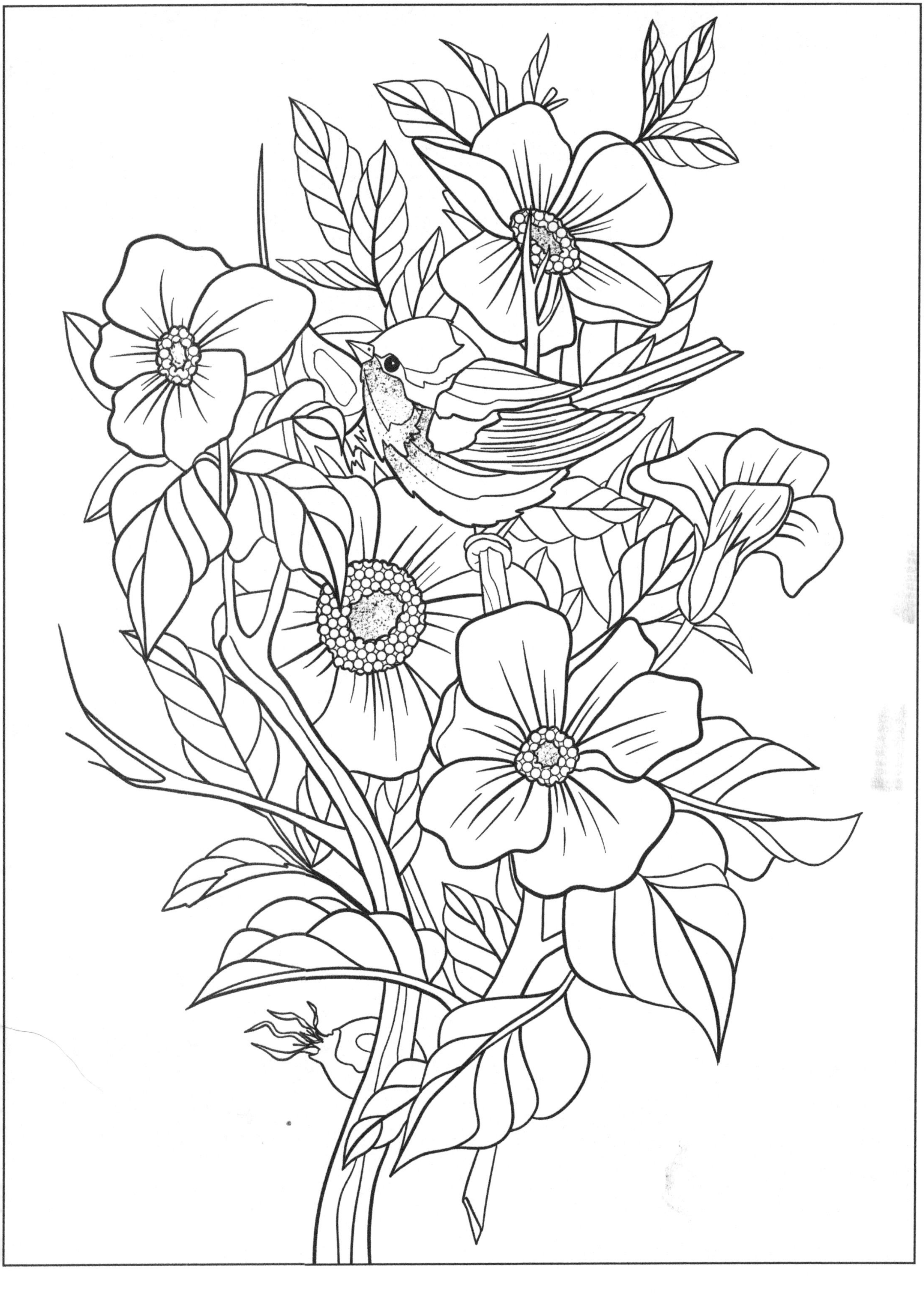

Inspirational Flower Quotes

"A flower blooming in the desert proves to the world that adversity, no matter how great, can be overcome."

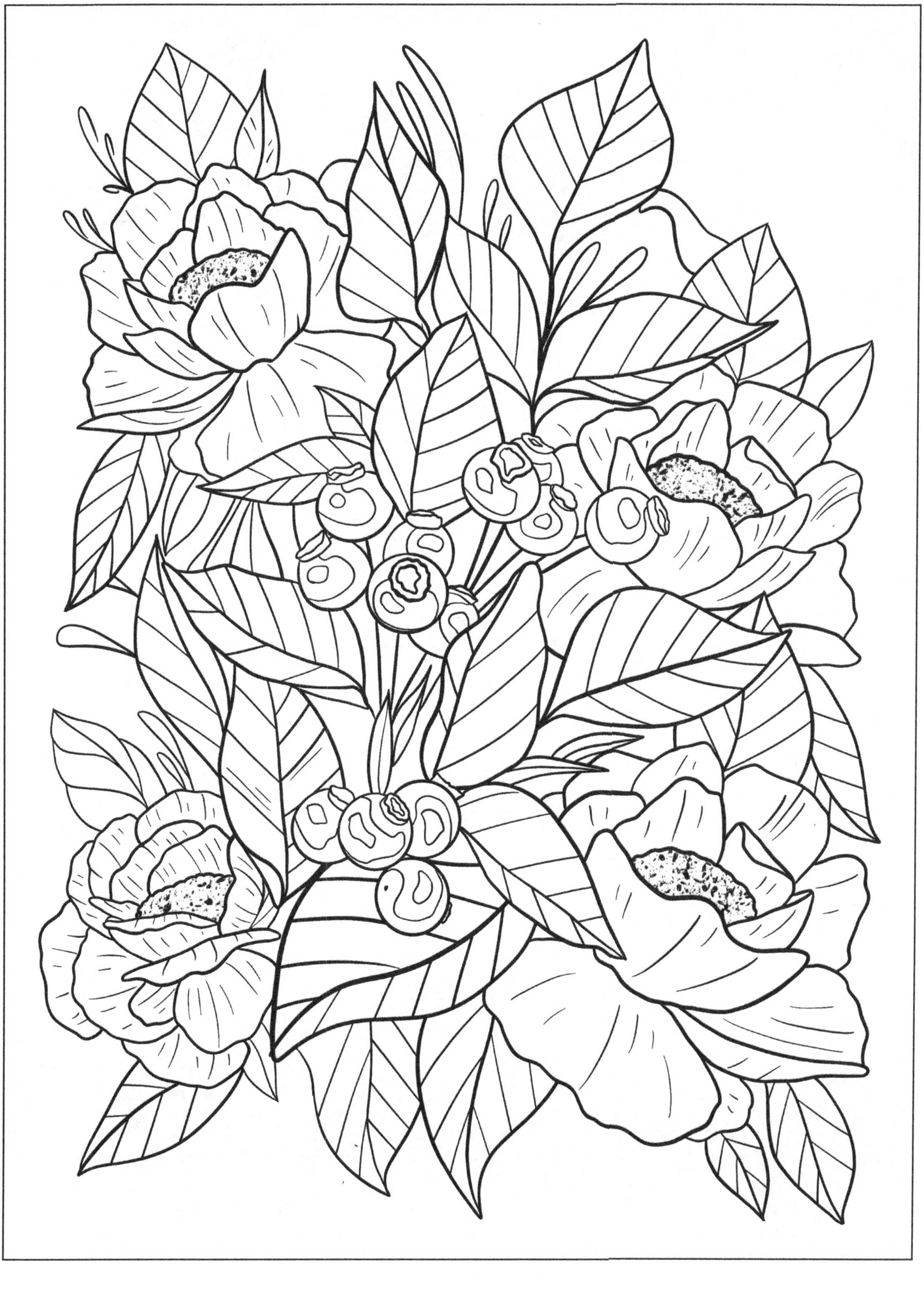

Inspirational Flower Quotes

"Like wildflowers; You must allow yourself to grow in all the places people thought you never would."

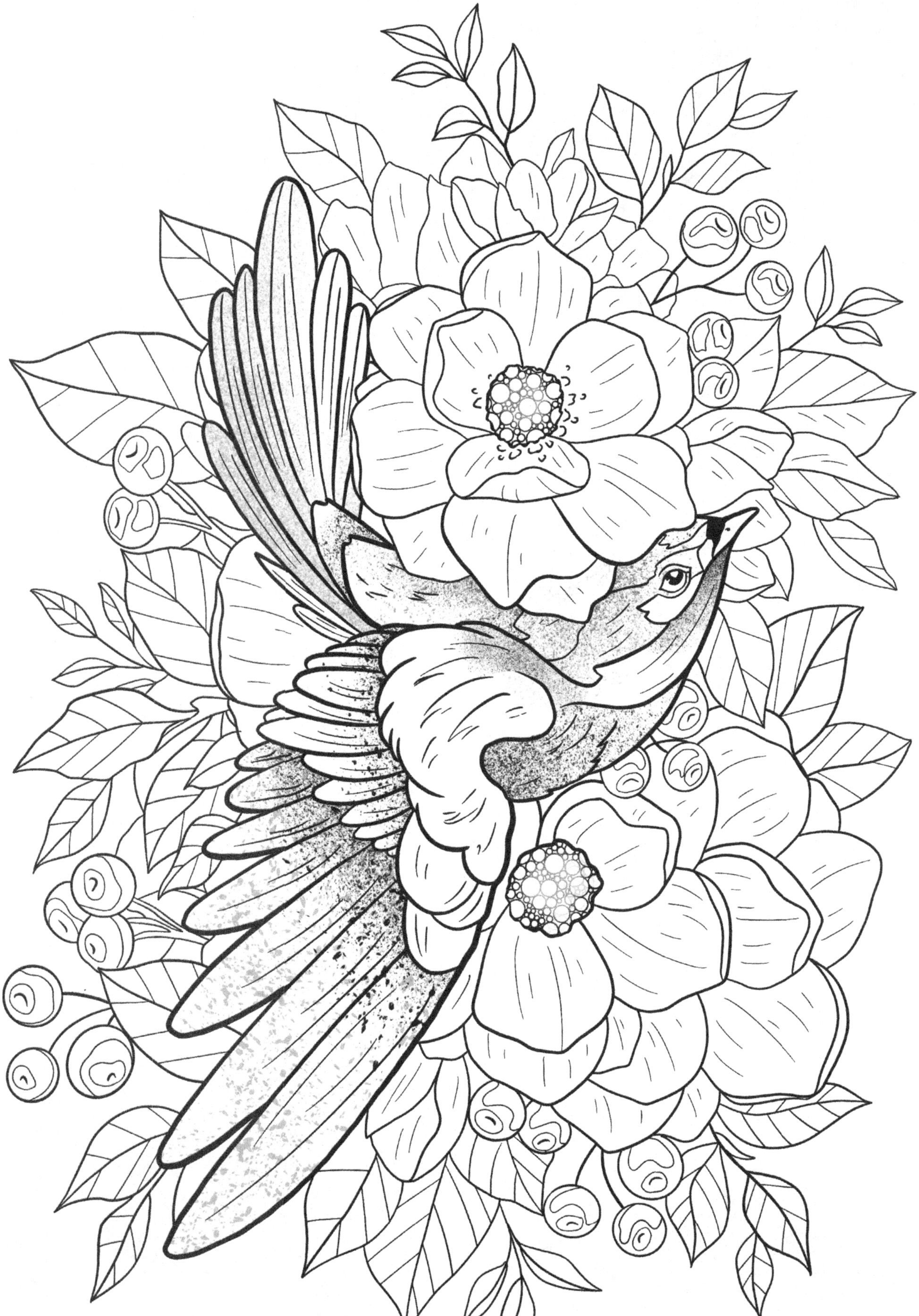

Inspirational Flower Quotes

"Don't wait for someone to bring you flowers. Plant your own garden and decorate your own soul."

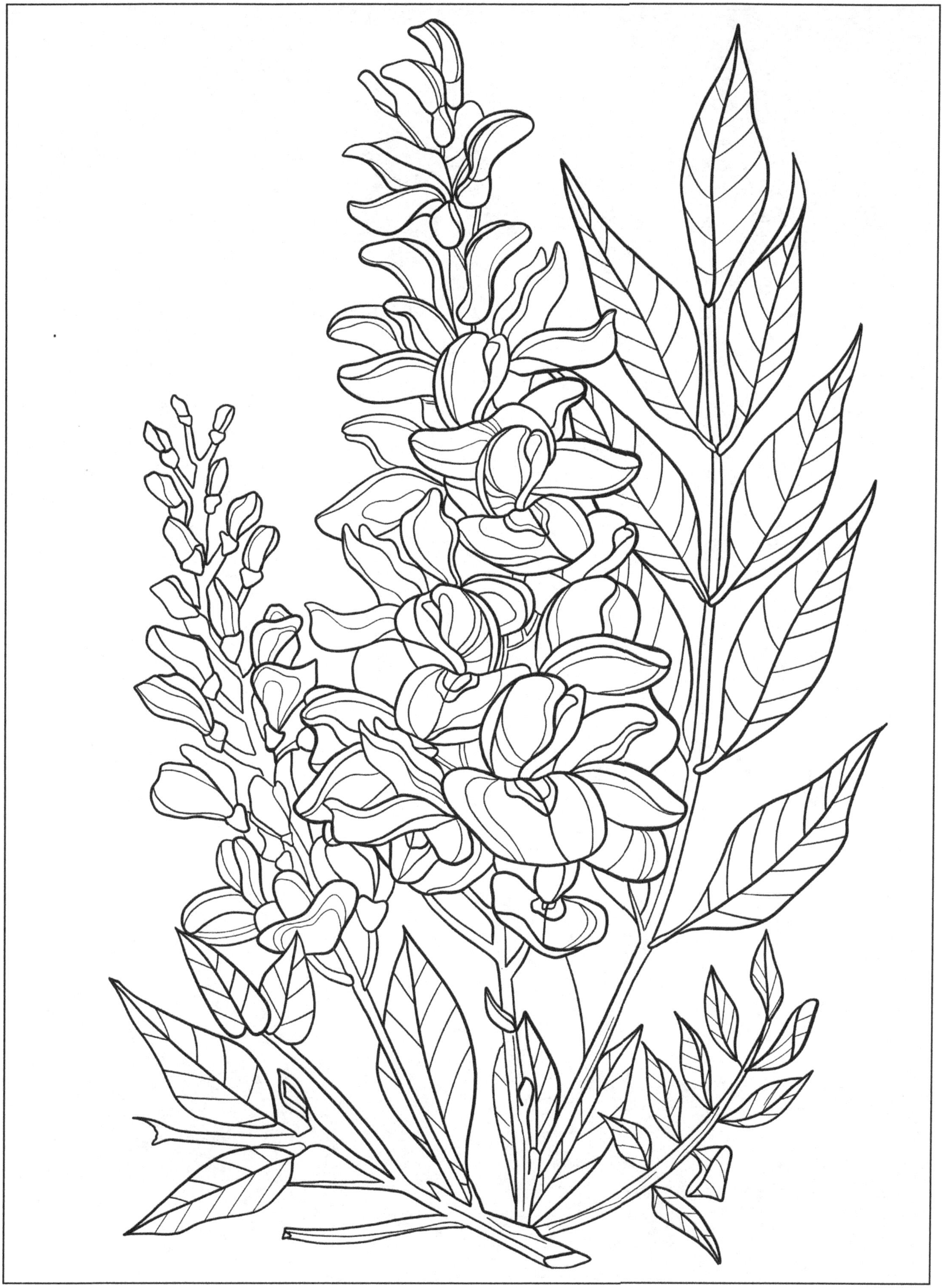

Inspirational Flower Quotes

"Politeness is the flower of humanity."

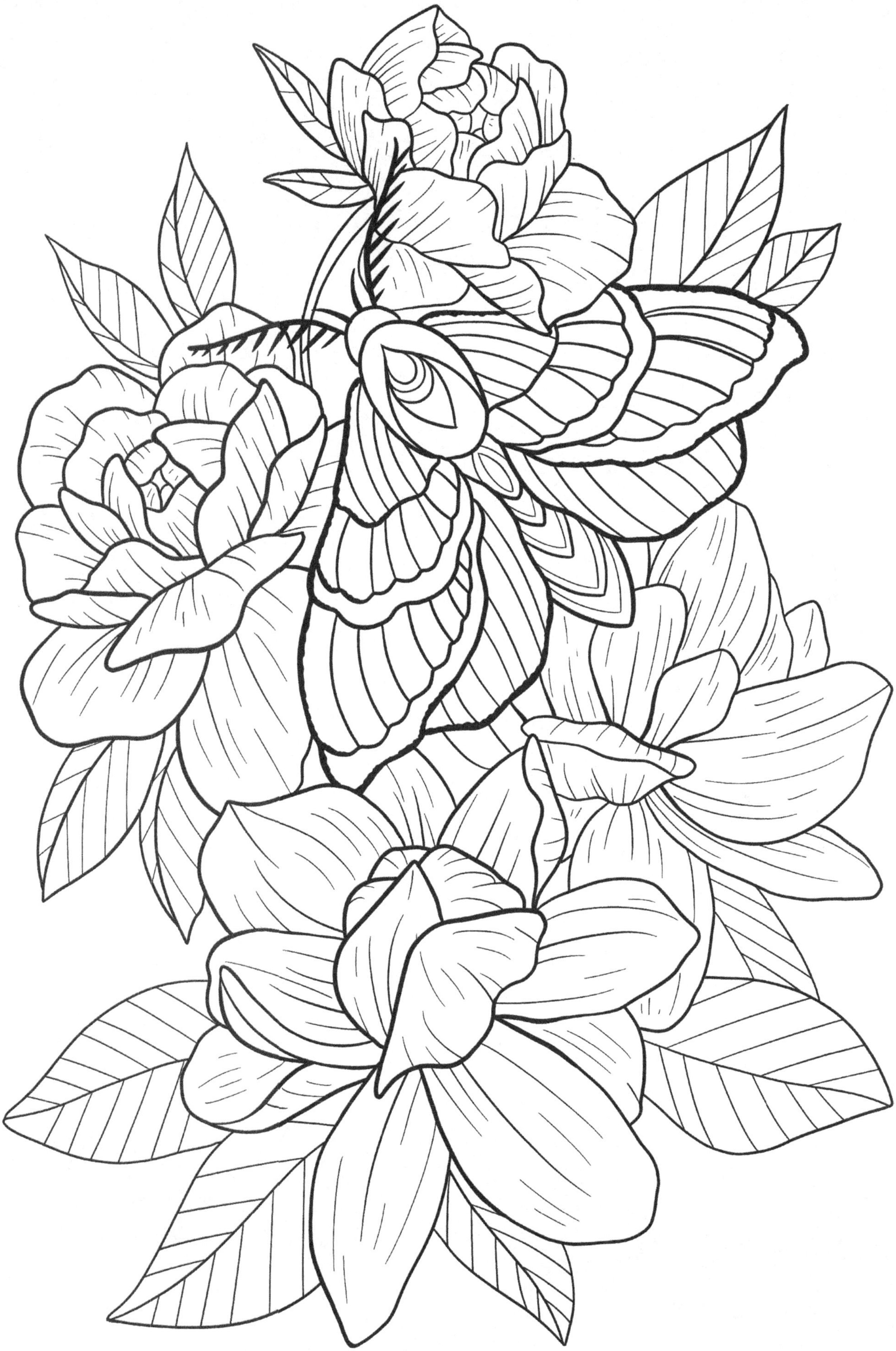

Inspirational Flower Quotes

"A flower does not use words to announce its arrival to the world; it just blooms."

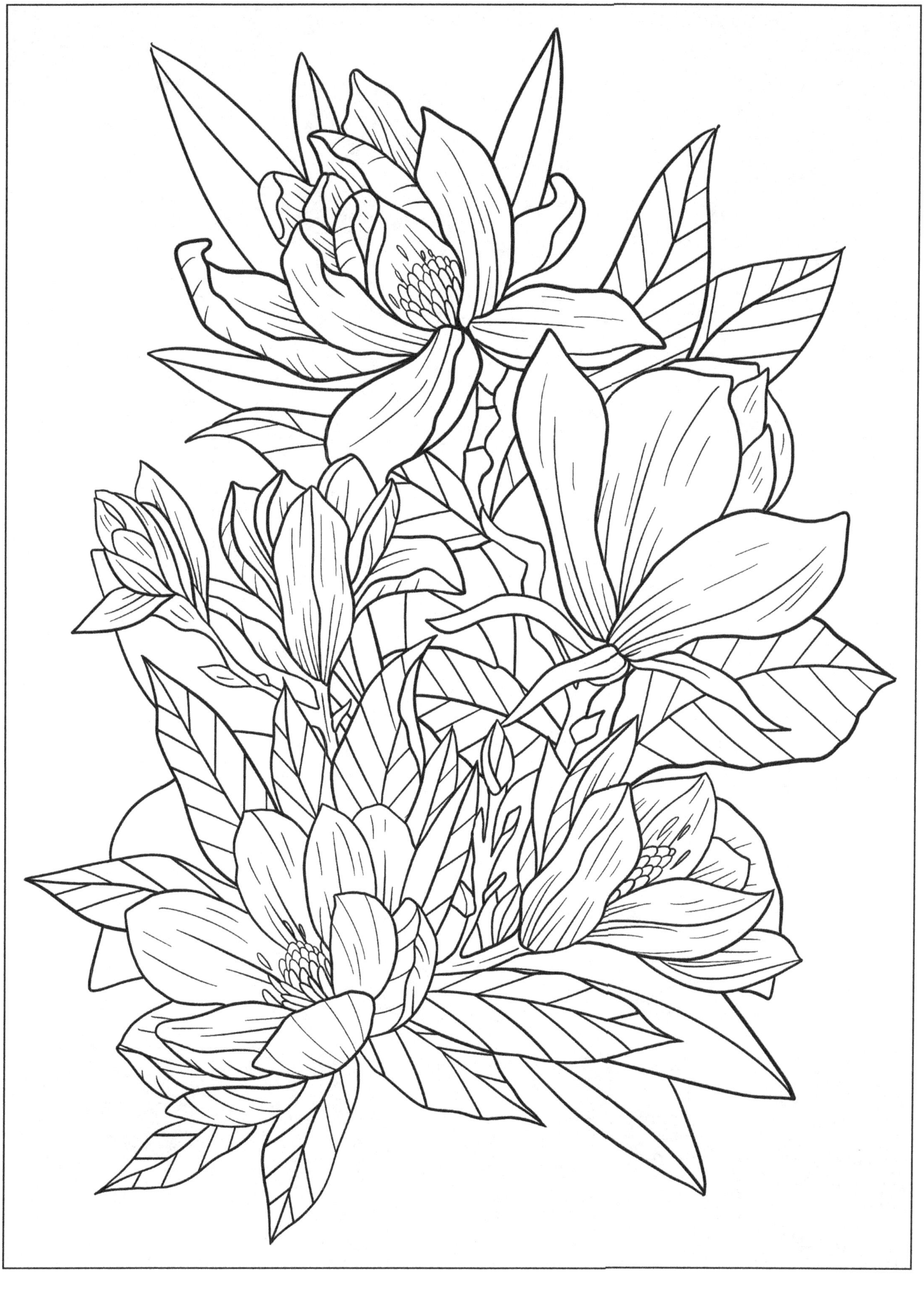

Inspirational Flower Quotes

"A rose can never be a sunflower, and a sunflower can never be a rose. All flowers are beautiful in their own way, and that's like women too."

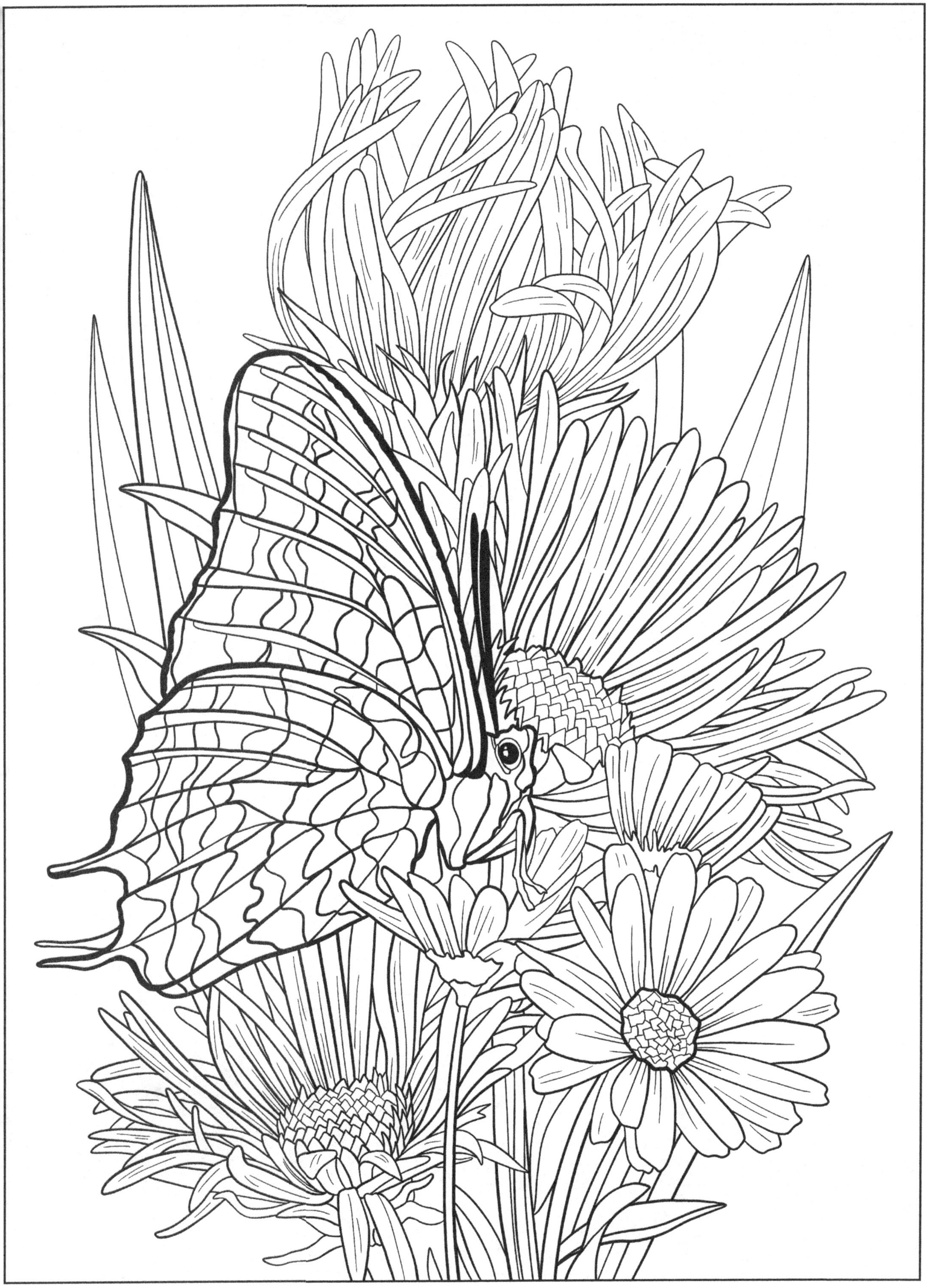

Inspirational Flower Quotes

"In joy and in sadness, flowers are our constant friends."

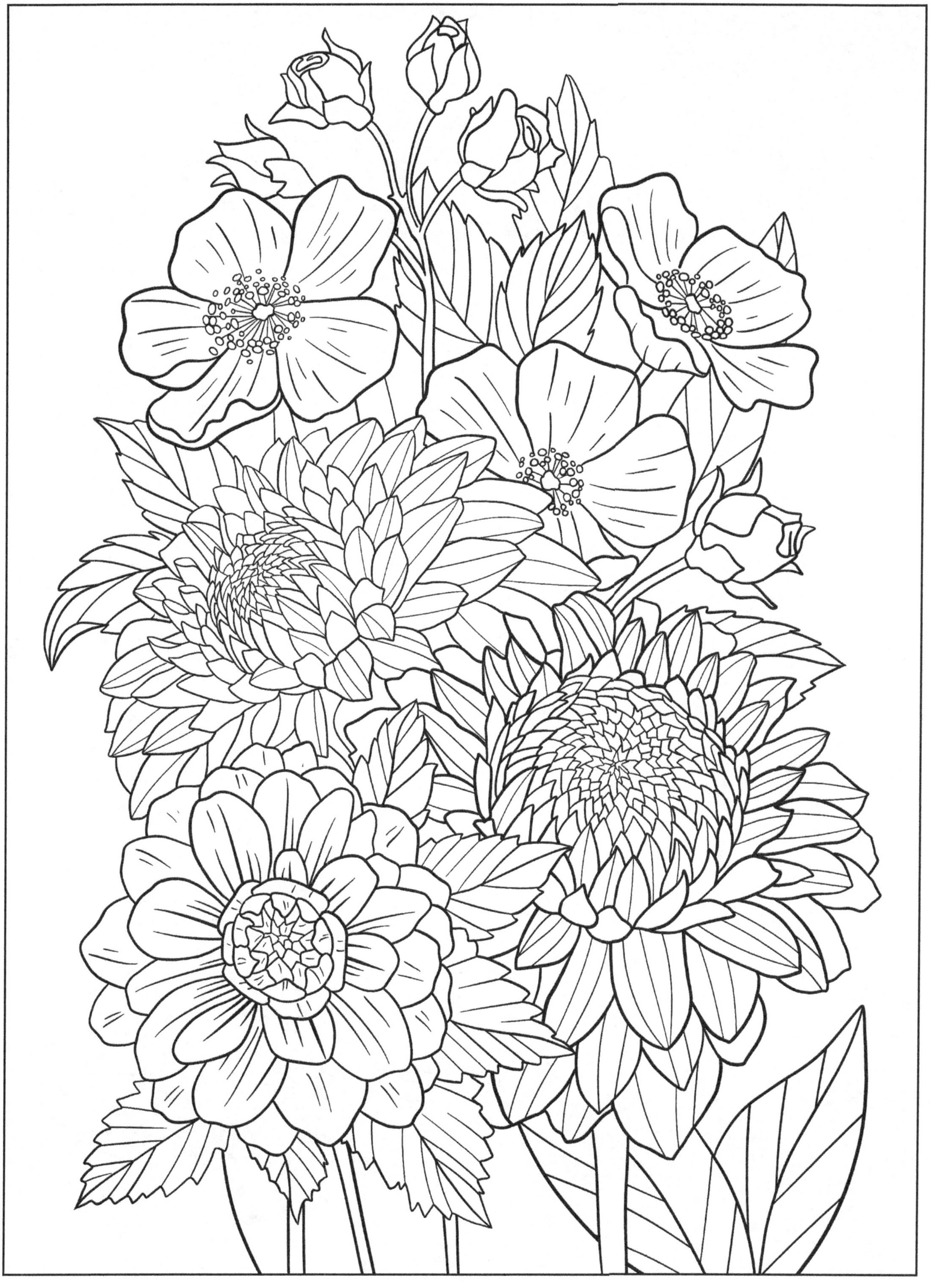

Inspirational Flower Quotes

"Many eyes go through the meadow, but few see the flowers in it."

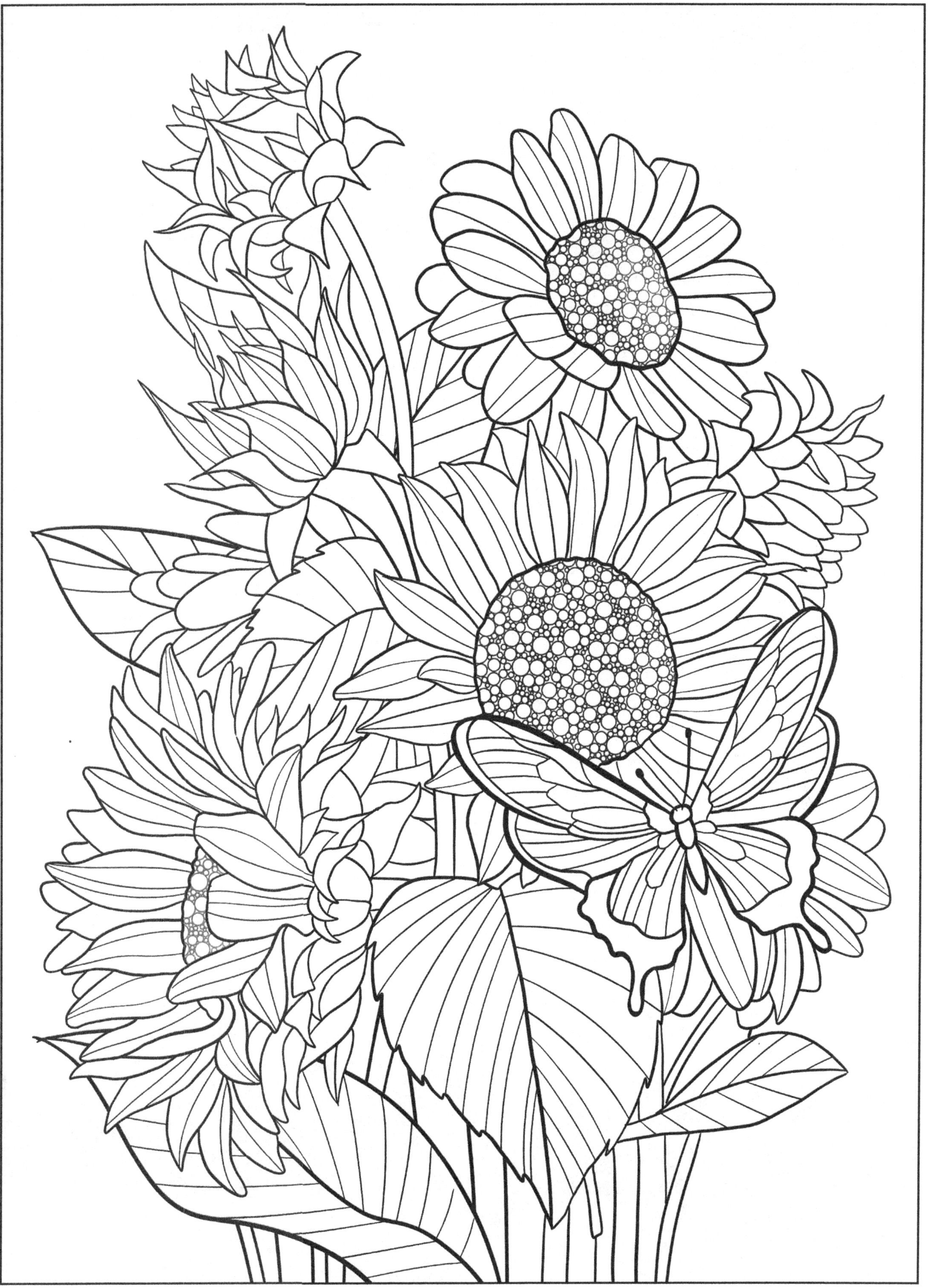

Inspirational Flower Quotes

"To plant a garden is to believe in tomorrow."

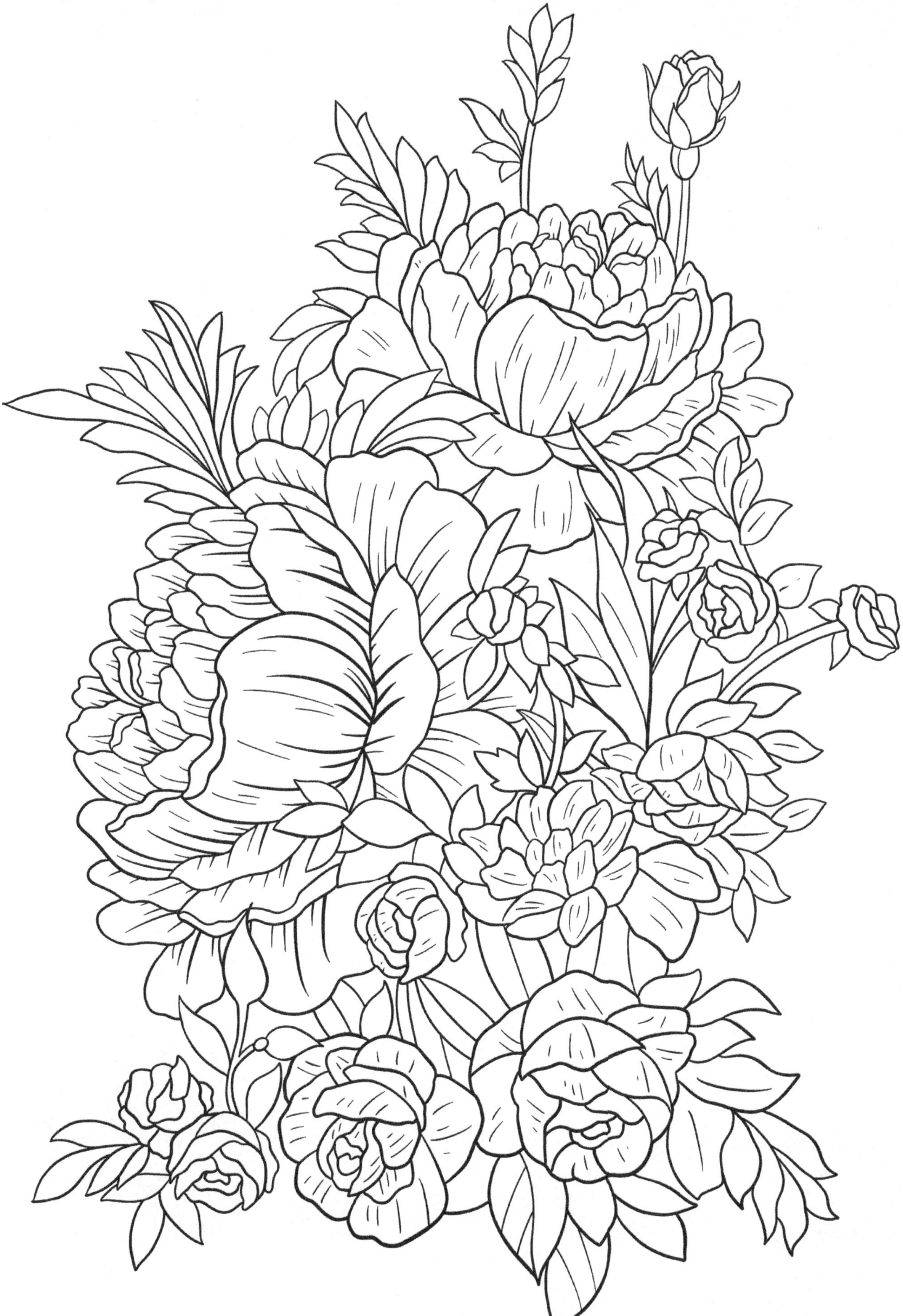

Inspirational Flower Quotes

"Don't let the tall weeds cast a shadow on the beautiful flowers in your garden."

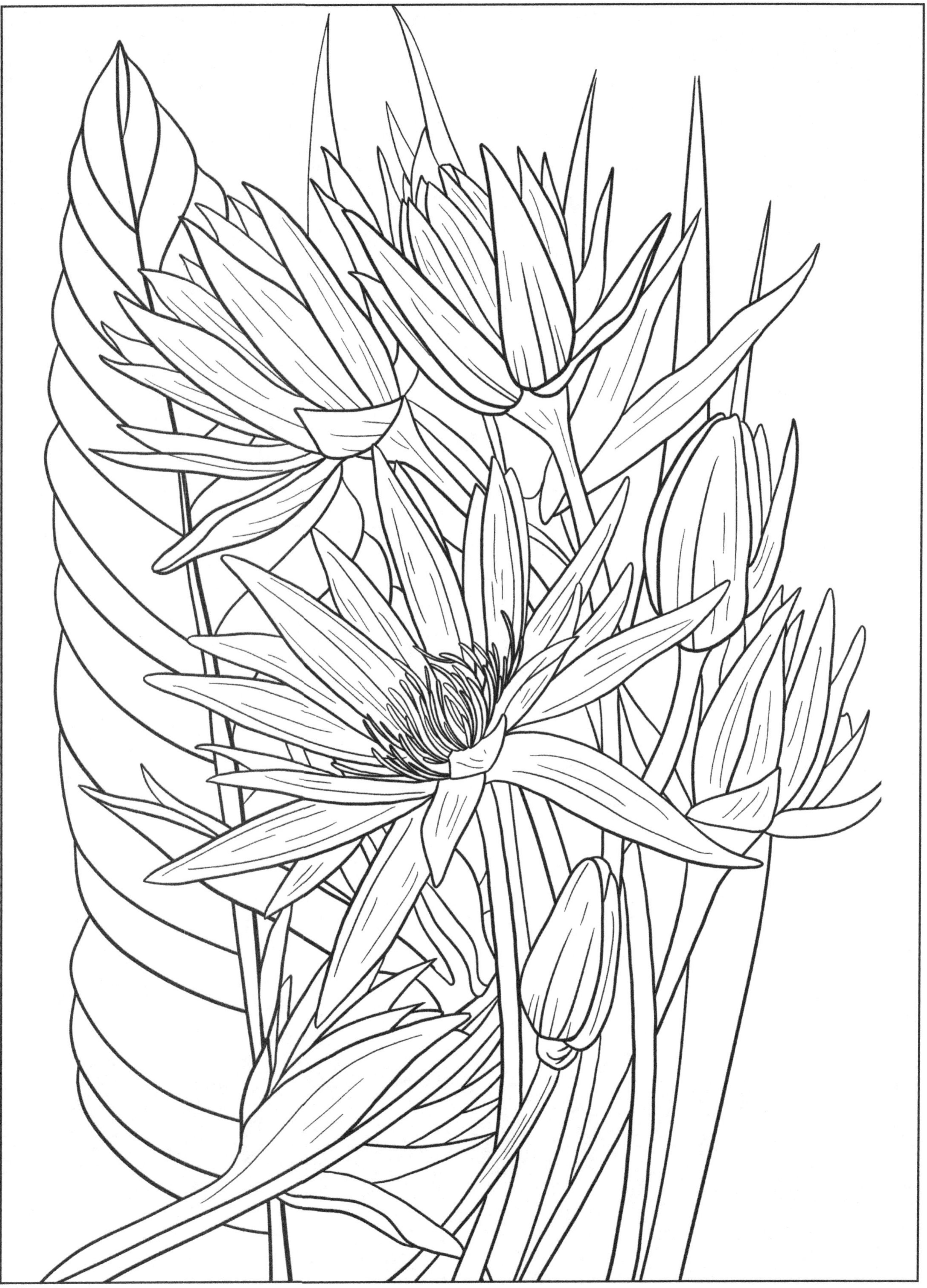

Inspirational Flower Quotes

"Flowers grow back, even after they are stepped on. So will I."

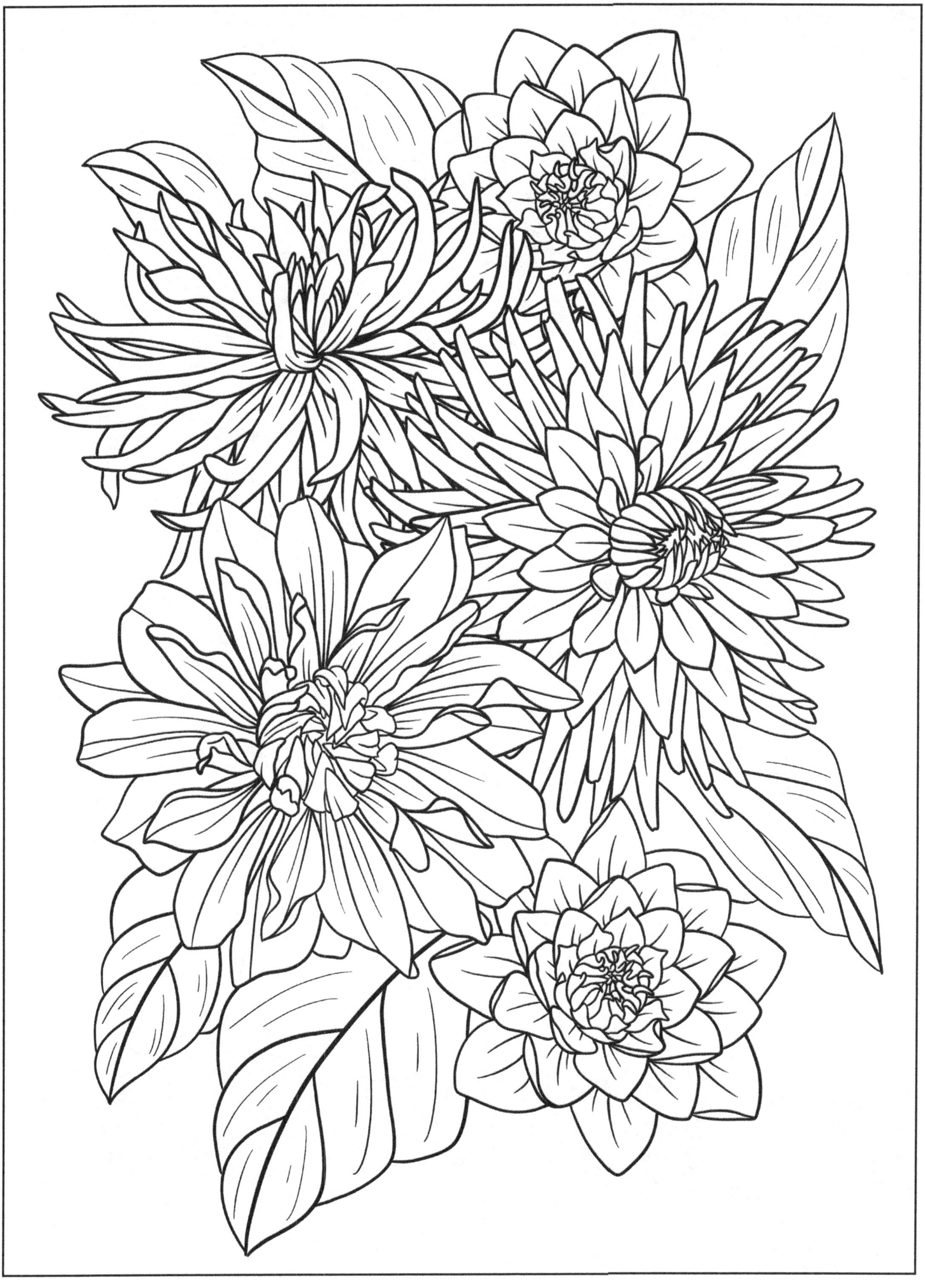

Inspirational Flower Quotes

"Spring: A lovely reminder of how beautiful change can truly be."

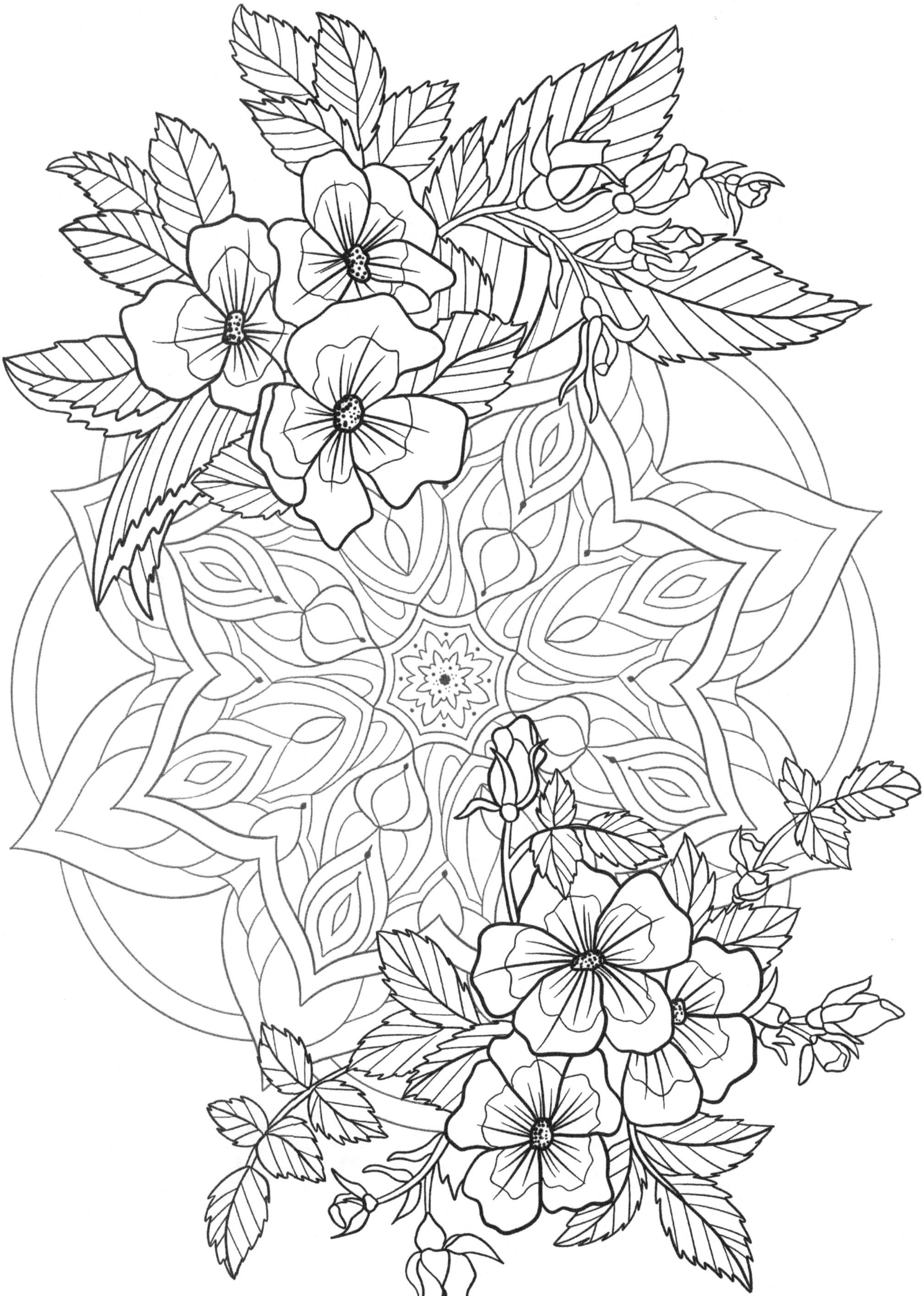

Inspirational Flower Quotes

"Gardens and flowers have a way of bringing people together, drawing them from their homes."

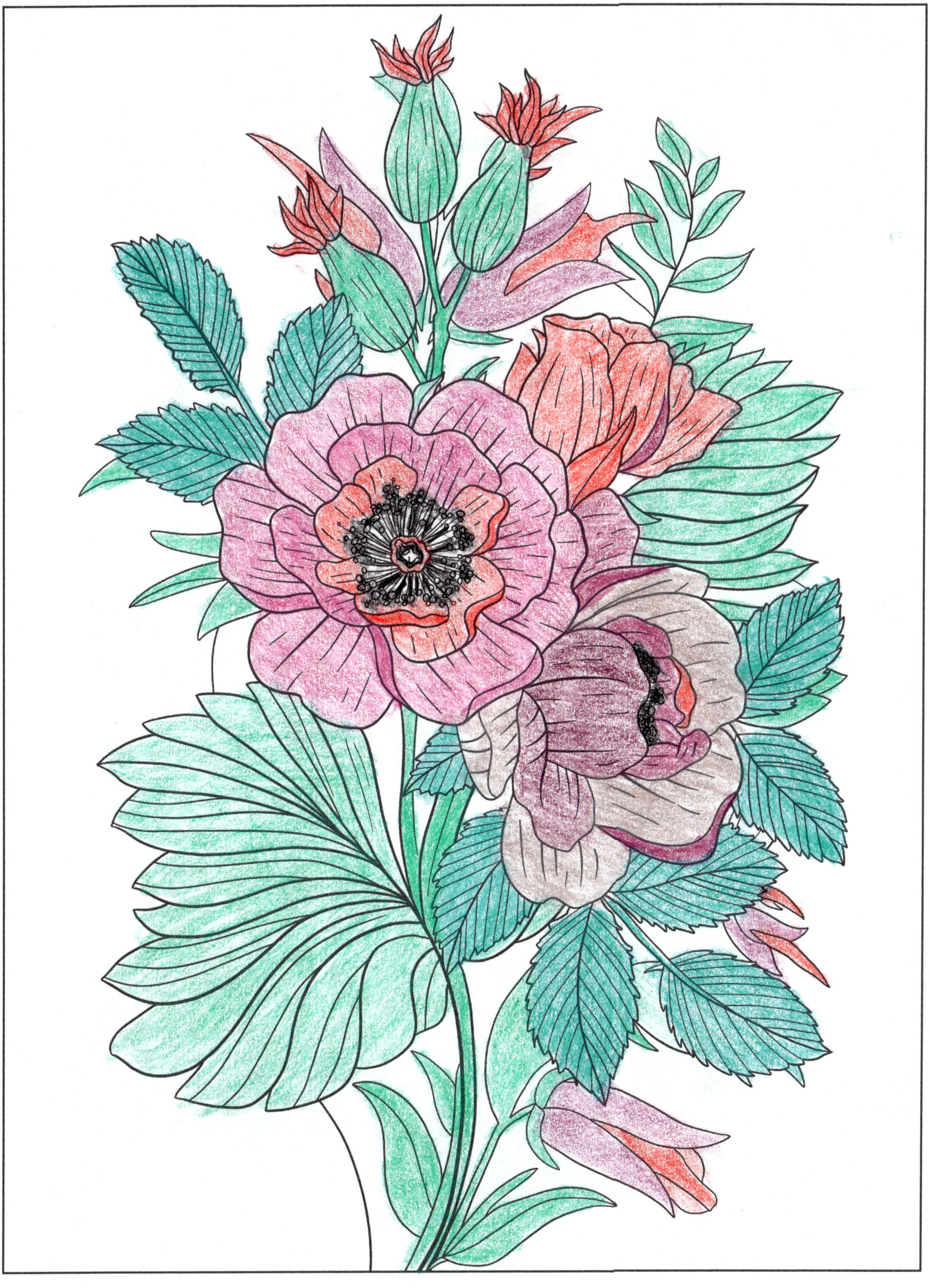

Inspirational Flower Quotes

"A flower does not use words to announce its arrival to the world; it just blooms."

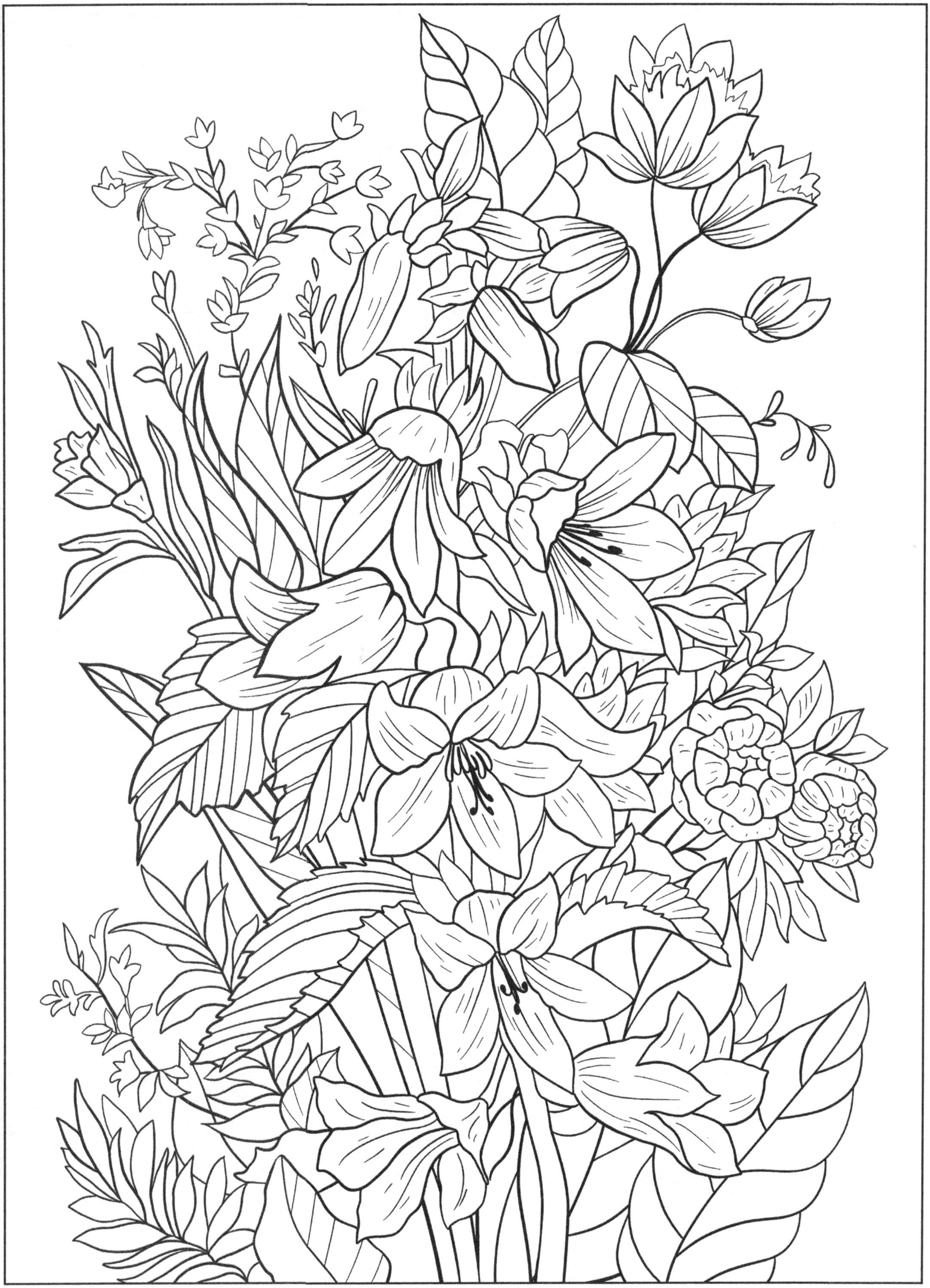

{ Inspirational Flower Quotes }

"A world of grief and pain flowers bloom— even then."

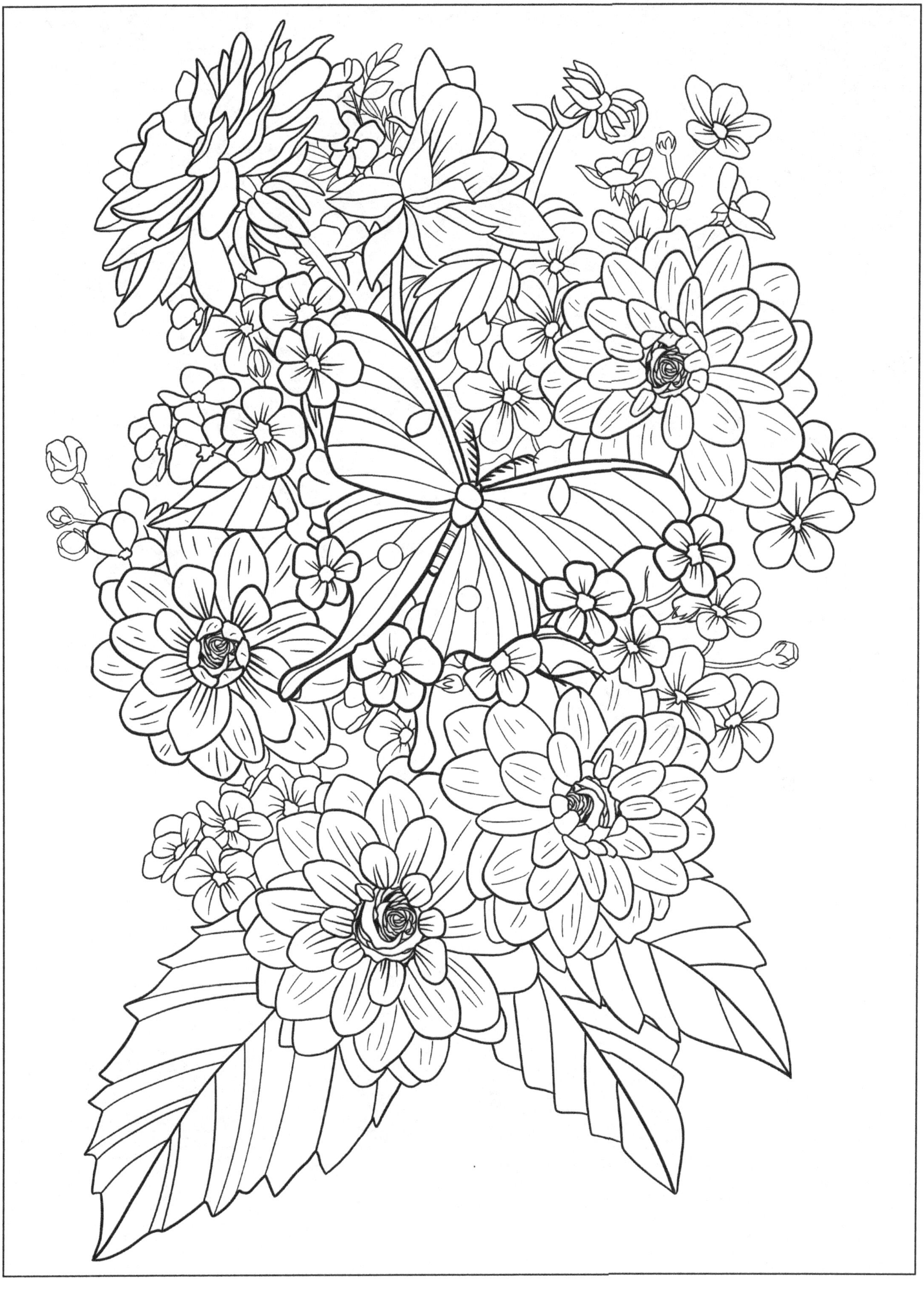

Inspirational Flower Quotes

"Happiness is to hold flowers in both hands."

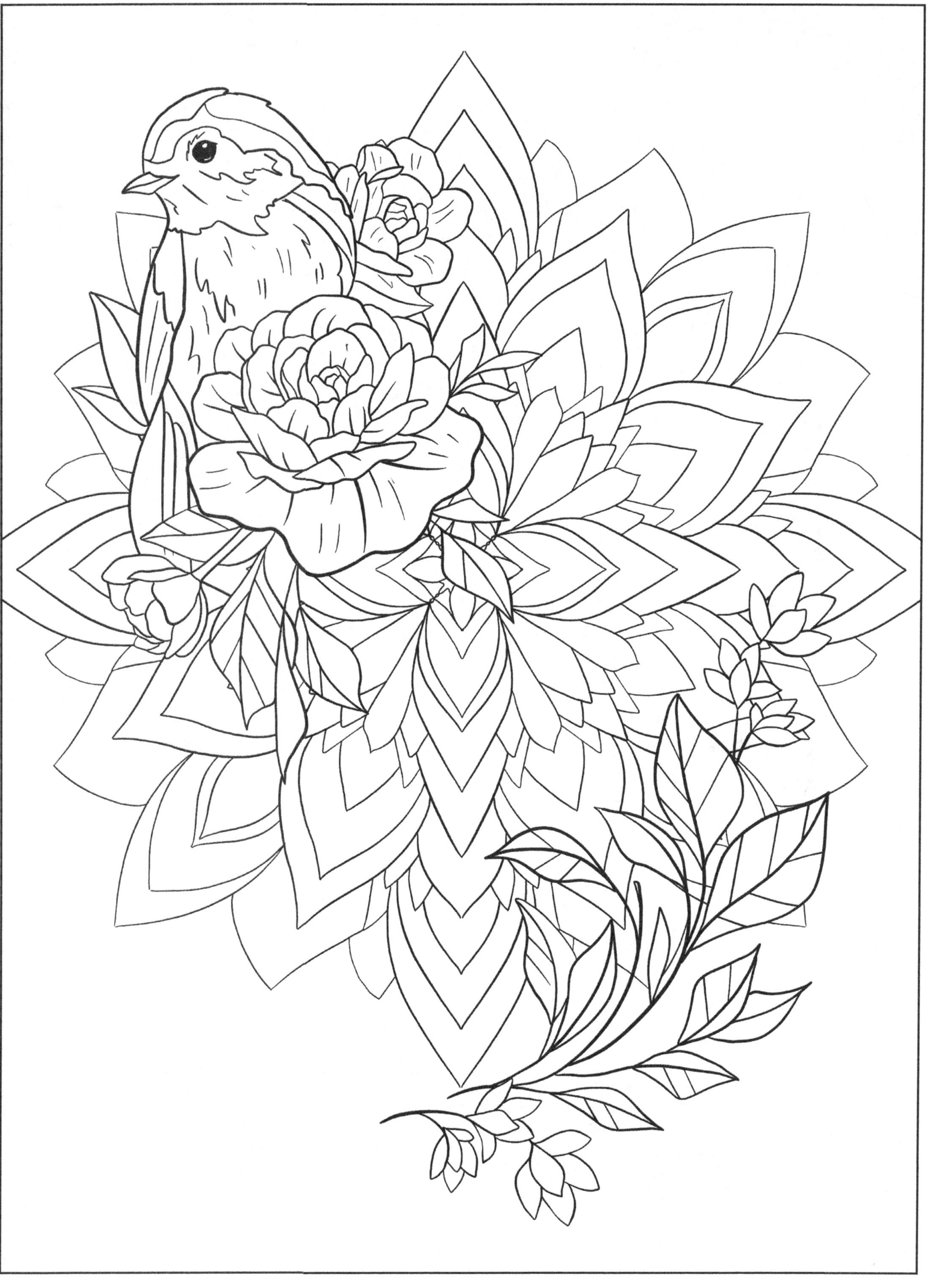

Inspirational Flower Quotes

"There are always flowers for those who want to see them"

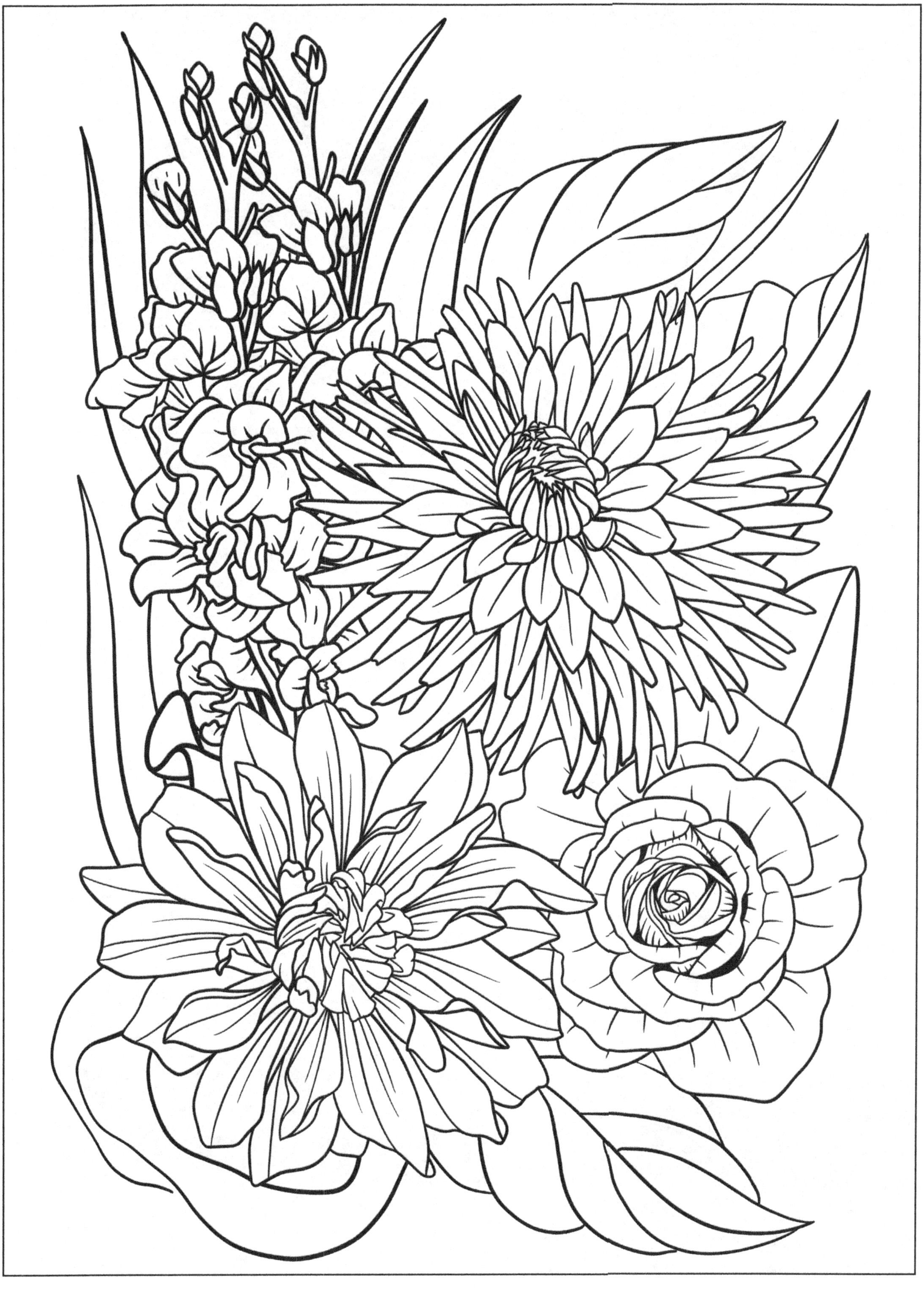

Inspirational Flower Quotes

"She wore flowers in her hair and carried magic secrets in her eyes."

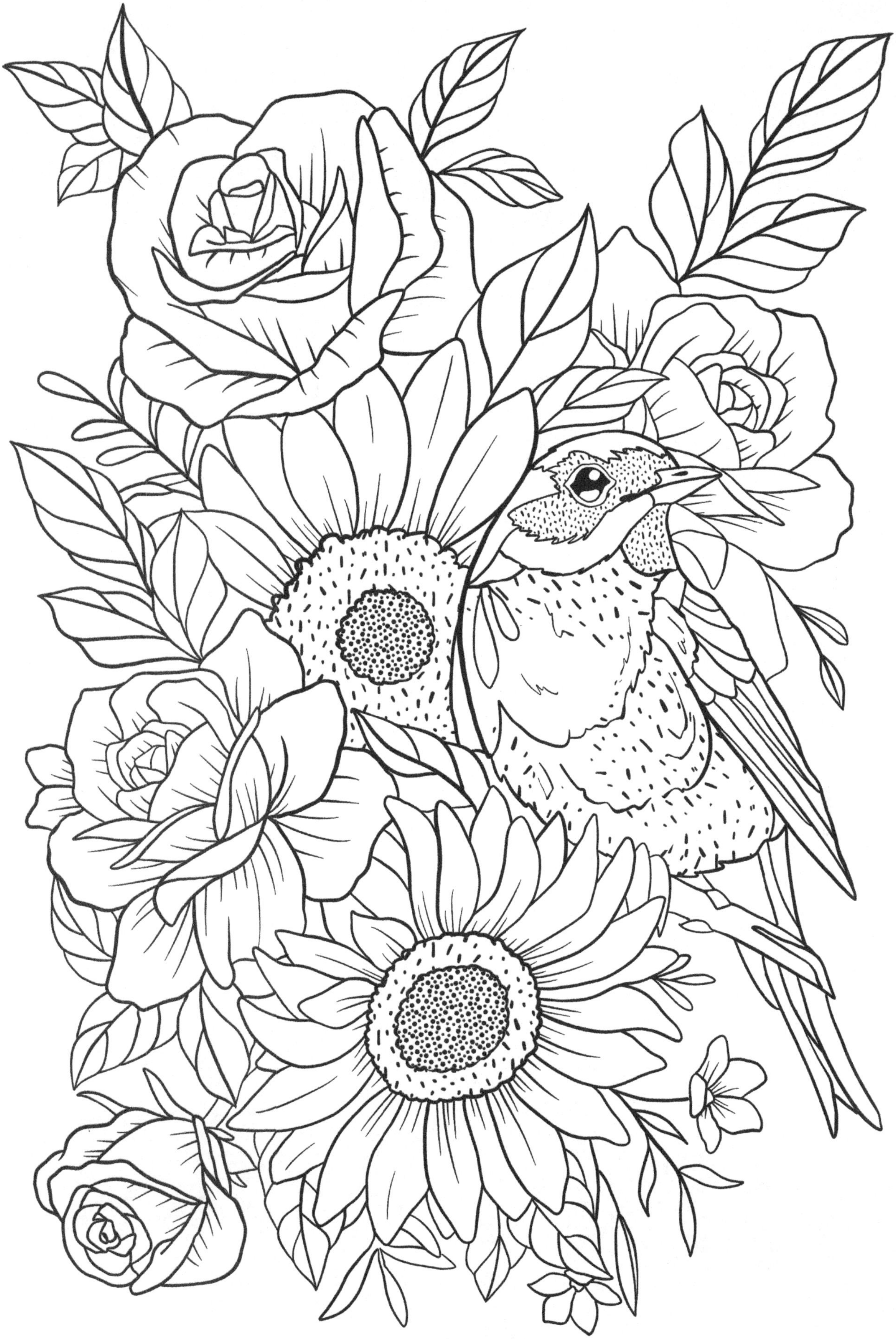

Happy Sophie Press

2022

Happy Sophie Press

Made in the USA
Monee, IL
05 January 2023